Financial Fun

Separating Truth from Myth

in Hilarious Fables

by Jimmy Glascott

Disclaimer:

Welcome to "Financial Fun: Separating Myth from Truth in Hilarious Fables"! Before delving into the gripping tales that lie within these pages, it is imperative that we set some boundaries and establish the purpose of this book.

Please note that the stories and anecdotes shared throughout this book are exclusively intended for information and entertainment purposes. They do not, repeat DO NOT, constitute financial advice or endorsements of any specific product or service.

While we strive to present accurate and reliable information, we cannot guarantee the absolute accuracy, completeness, or timeliness of the narratives. Moreover, any resemblance to actual persons or events is purely coincidental and not intended to harm or offend.

We strongly advise against interpreting the content of this book as sound guidance or recommendations for financial decision-making. Always consult with a qualified professional before making any financial choices. The ideas shared in this book are purely fictional and should not be applied in real-life situations without the appropriate knowledge and expertise.

By immersing yourself in the amusing tales found within this book, you acknowledge and accept that you are solely responsible for your financial decisions and actions. The author, publisher, and any individuals associated with this book bear no liability for any consequences arising from misinterpretation or misuse of the information provided.

So sit back, relax, and enjoy the playful world of "Financial Fun: Separating Myth from Truth in Hilarious Fables," but do keep in mind that these stories are purely meant for your entertainment and not as a substitute for professional financial advice.

Happy reading!

Introduction

In "Financial Fun: Separating Myth from Truth in Hilarious Fables," Franklin and Olivia invite you to join them on their uproarious adventures as they debunk financial fallacies with wit, humor, and a dash of sarcasm. Get ready for a rollercoaster ride that will tickle your funny bone while you learn invaluable lessons about money management.

From decoding the enigma of compound interest to demystifying the intricate art of budgeting, this book weaves an unforgettable tapestry of laughter and financial wisdom. Meet a cast of delightfully flawed characters who find themselves trapped in hilarious predicaments, teaching you valuable lessons along the way. Watch as a romance blossoms between a spendthrift squirrel and a thrifty mouse, revealing the importance of impulse control and saving for the future.

Prepare to chuckle as an overconfident bull and a pessimistic bear engage in a debate about market predictability, shedding light on the complexity of investing. Discover the perils of falling prey to get-rich-quick schemes through the misadventures of a misguided hare who finds out that "cryptocurrency" isn't exactly a hidden treasure buried in the digital world.

In each fable, author and financial guru, Felix Moneybags, imparts his expertise in a way that is accessible, relatable, and a little bit cheeky. With lessons wrapped in laughter, these fables take dull financial truths and transform them into rib-tickling tales that will leave you enlightened and entertained.

So, dear reader, put on your thinking cap and get ready for an engaging journey through the realm of finances. Whether you are a seasoned investor, a recent graduate, or simply someone who wants to make better financial choices, "Financial Fun" is your passport to decoding the secrets of money with a light-hearted twist.

Remember, life is too short to be bored by finance! Prepare to be captivated, educated, and thoroughly amused by this unique blend of comedy and financial education. Your thrilling adventure awaits – grab a copy of "Financial Fun" and embark on a journey where myths crumble, truths prevail, and laughter is the rightful ruler of the financial kingdom.

And so, dear readers, remember Penny's tale. Budgeting may sound dull, but with a dash of creativity, laughter, and a trusty Mr. Spreadsheet by your side, you can turn financial planning into an adventure filled with squirrel-sized triumphs. Embrace the power of budgeting, and you too can have a prosperous and oh-so-fun life in the exciting realm of finances!

Contents

Chapter One: The Magic Wand Illusion: Dispelling Wealth Myths in Hilarious Fables

Once upon a time, in the bustling kingdom of Coinlandia, there lived a magician named Prestorius. Now Prestorius, while being quite gifted in the art of illusion, was known for his obsession with finding the secret to unlimited wealth. He believed that the key to this prosperity lay in a magnificent and elusive artifact known as the Magic Wand, said to grant its possessor untold riches. Ah yes, the Magic Wand, a treasure that had captured the imaginations of countless dreamers, including our dear Prestorius.

One fine day, Prestorius embarked on an epic quest to find the fabled wand and prove that it possessed the power to transform one's fortunes. Armed with his quick wit and a vast collection of magical tricks, he ventured into the deep, enchanted forest that guarded the treasures of Coinlandia.

As our magician journeyed further into the forest, he stumbled upon a peculiar creature known as the Wealthy Raccoon. This raccoon, known far and wide for its cunning ability to navigate complex financial systems, had amassed great wealth over the years. Prestorius, upon spotting the raccoon, couldn't help but feel a rush of excitement.

"Ah, esteemed raccoon," Prestorius called out, tipping his hat. "I am Prestorius, the great magician. I come in search of the Magic Wand to bring prosperity to my humble life. Will you help me find it?"

The Wealthy Raccoon raised an eyebrow, softly chuckling. "Ah, dear Prestorius, you are on an amusing quest, indeed. But let me share a fable that may illuminate the truth you seek." And with those words, the raccoon gestured for the magician to follow, leading him deep into the forest.

As they walked, the Wealthy Raccoon shared the tale of a talented blacksmith named Bernard. Bernard, skilled as he was, believed that the Magic Wand held the secret to his financial triumphs. Day and night, he forged enchanted weapons, eagerly searching for the wand's appearance. People from all corners of the kingdom flocked to Bernard's shop, desperate to purchase one of his "magical" blades, hoping for a shortcut to their wealth.

The raccoon paused, and with a sly grin, continued the tale. "But here's the twist, my dear Prestorius. Bernard's blades were indeed magical, but not in the way people expected. They couldn't magically grant wealth but rather were imbued with a bewitching charm that made the wielder work harder, smarter, and more diligently."

Prestorius scratched his head, bewildered. "So, the magical blades didn't create riches out of thin air?"

The Wealthy Raccoon chuckled. "Nothing as miraculous, I'm afraid. Wealth, dear Prestorius, rarely appears simply by waving a wand. It is the product of dedication, patience, and finding value in serving others. These are the true keys to financial success."

As Prestorius reflected on this revelation, they arrived at a clearing where a wise owl named Wisebert was presiding over a

2

meeting of Coinlandia's most prosperous creatures.

"Ah, Wisebert," declared the raccoon, "I bring to you Prestorius, the great magician who seeks the Magic Wand."

Wisebert, with a twinkle in her eyes, surveyed Prestorius. "Dear magician, if wealth were something conjured by a mere twist of a wand, would it not be found everywhere? True prosperity comes not from magical artifacts but from nurturing skills, adapting to change, and seizing opportunities presented through hard work and calculated risk."

Prestorius sighed, realizing that he had been chasing the wrong dream all along. "You're right, Wisebert. It seems I've been too focused on the magic and not enough on the effort it takes to build true wealth."

And so, Prestorius bid farewell to the Wealthy Raccoon and Wisebert, etching these invaluable lessons into his memory. With a renewed sense of purpose, he returned to the kingdom of Coinlandia, ready to share his newfound wisdom and enthusiasm for financial success through simple, honest means.

And thus, dear readers, Prestorius embarked on a different kind of magic — the magic of action, dedication, and the belief that true wealth lies not in the wand but within ourselves.
So, next time you find yourself yearning for a magic wand, remember the tale of Prestorius, and let his journey remind you that the true key to financial success lies not in a mythical artifact but in the intangible qualities that reside within.

Chapter Two: The Story of Penny the Procrastinator

Once upon a time in a small town there lived a lively squirrel named Penny. Penny was known for her endless energy and her incredible talent for collecting acorns. She spent her days happily gathering nuts and storing them in her cozy treehouse.

Now, Penny had a reputation for being a bit of a procrastinator. She would often forget to plan for the long, cold winter months that lay ahead. Penny would spend her acorns whimsically, splurging on the latest squirrel fashion trends and delicious gourmet acorn delicacies.

One sunny day, as Penny frolicked in the forest, she stumbled upon a seminar hosted by Wise Old Owl. Intrigued, Penny decided to join the gathering of woodland creatures, hoping to learn something useful.

Wise Old Owl explained the importance of budgeting and the perils of Penny's habits. He shared tales of squirrels with empty pantries and cold bellies in the middle of winter because they didn't plan ahead. The crowd gasped, some glancing warily at Penny.

Humiliated and eager to make amends, Penny approached the Wise Old Owl after the seminar. "Oh, Wise Old Owl, I am guilty of careless acorn spending and lack of budgeting. What shall I do?"

The Wise Old Owl, with a glint in his eyes, quipped, "Fear not, young Penny! I have just the solution for you. Meet Mr. Spreadsheet, the Master of Budgeting!"

Penny's eyes widened as a dapper little squirrel with a pocket protector and an impressive collection of calculators stepped forward. "Greetings, Penny! I am Mr. Spreadsheet, and I'm here to save the day," he declared, adjusting his glasses.

Together with Mr. Spreadsheet, Penny embarked on a hilarious journey of budgeting enlightenment. They constructed a budget treehouse, complete with acorn compartments for expenses and savings. Penny diligently tracked her acorn income and expenses, discovering that fancy designer acorn hats cost a lot more than they were worth.

Along the way, Penny encountered her mischievous friend, Rusty the Raccoon, who was notorious for his lavish spending habits. Rusty threw wild parties and showered his friends with gifts, oblivious to the reckless drain on his acorn resources.

Laughing heartily, Penny invited Rusty to join her budgeting adventure. She explained how her newfound budgeting skills allowed her to spend wisely, save for the future, and enjoy life while being financially responsible.

The trio of Penny, Mr. Spreadsheet, and Rusty started a support group called "Save with Squirrels," helping woodland creatures across the forest overcome their budgeting blind spots. With clever charts, amusing anecdotes, and some squirrely dance moves, they taught others how to resist the temptation of impulse acorn purchases and build a solid financial foundation.

As the seasons changed, the woodland creatures witnessed the transformations in Penny and Rusty. Penny had a full pantry and even invested some acorns in a tree bark spa, enjoying luxurious squirrel massages under the gentle paws of trained professionals.

In the end, Penny and Rusty not only learned the value of budgeting but also discovered a sense of inner peace and security that came with financial responsibility. They turned their budgeting journey into a musical called "The Nutty Numbers," which became a hit across the forest, spreading the message of financial sensibility with catchy songs and squirrelly dances.

Once upon a time, in a land where numbers ruled and dollars reigned, there lived a clever fox named Franklin and a wise owl named Olivia. Together, they embarked on a daring journey through financial forests filled with deceitful rumors and money myths.

Chapter 3: The Adventures of Mr. Risky and Dr. Cautious

Once upon a time, in the land of Financia, there lived two friends with contrasting views on money. Mr. Risky, a flamboyant daredevil who enjoyed the thrill of investing, and Dr. Cautious, a meticulous saver who trusted only in the safety of his piggy bank. Despite their differences, they shared a curiosity for the concept of risk tolerance.

One sunny morning, as they sipped tea in Mr. Risky's treehouse, with its balcony overlooking the bustling city, they began their whimsical journey to understand the true meaning of risk tolerance.

"You see, Dr. Cautious," Mr. Risky exclaimed, waving his arms with excitement. "Risk is like playing on a giant teeter-totter. You can either go all the way up and enjoy the thrill of the ride or stay at the bottom, where it's safe but dull!"

Dr. Cautious, who barely managed to balance his teacup, raised an eyebrow. "I beg to differ, Mr. Risky. Risk is more like walking a tightrope. It's about finding the perfect equilibrium between caution and adventure."

With these analogies in mind, they set off on their first escapade to the mystical Wall Street Wizard Academy. There, they met a wise old professor named Professor Insightful, who promised to teach them about assessing risk.

"Welcome, my brave learners!" Professor Insightful boomed, wearing colorful robes adorned with charts and graphs. "Today, we shall learn about the dangers of the penny-pinching dragon!"

In a grand gesture, he summoned a dragon made entirely of shiny pennies, which unleashed a fiery sneeze, scattering them in every direction. Mr. Risky and Dr. Cautious made a wild dash, trying to catch as many pennies as possible.

"This is your risk tolerance test!" Professor Insightful laughed. "The more you collect, the higher your tolerance!"

Mr. Risky, completely absorbed in catching the coins, slipped and fell—sprouting a slightly charred tail.

"See, Mr. Risky, your adventurous spirit led you astray!" Dr. Cautious chuckled, extending a helping hand.

Brushing off his singed feathers, Mr. Risky grinned. "True, but fortune favors the brave, my friend."

Their next misadventure brought them to the quirky Money Maze, a labyrinth of financial decisions. Two paths lay before them: one representing high-risk investments, and the other steady yet low returns.

"Choose wisely, my friends," a melodious voice sang from above. "Remember, without risk, there can be no reward!"

Mr. Risky dashed toward the high-risk path, jumping over the obstacles, and laughing as gilded treasures fell into his hands. Meanwhile, Dr. Cautious cautiously tiptoed on the low-risk path, gathering modest but stable rewards.

At the end of their paths, they met at a golden chest. Their rewards were starkly different – Mr. Risky had gathered peacock feathers and a medallion shaped like a bull, while Dr. Cautious held a modest key made of silver.

Although Mr. Risky sported his peacock feathers proudly, he couldn't help but admire the simplicity of Dr. Cautious's key.

"Ah, Dr. Cautious, you may not have garnered the largest treasure, but your stability is admirable," Mr. Risky confessed, twirling a peacock feather.

Dr. Cautious smiled. "Indeed, my friend. Luck may favor the bold, but consistency triumphs in the end."

As their whimsical adventures unfolded, Mr. Risky and Dr. Cautious began to understand the importance of risk assessment. They realized managing risks was like taming unicorns or juggling flaming bananas – a delicate balance of fun and careful planning.

Together, they concluded that the key to financial success was understanding one's risk tolerance, to neither be a reckless adventurer nor a timid hoarder. Through their lively escapades, readers learned that risk was not something to fear but rather a crucial ingredient for achieving their dreams.

And so, Mr. Risky and Dr. Cautious continued their adventures, inspiring others to seek their own financial whimsies while treading the line between thrilling risks and careful calculations.

For in the realm of finance, when approached with a smile and a touch of clever thinking, even the most daunting risks could be conquered with laughter.

Chapter 4: The Tale of Two Squirrels and the Acorn Showdown

Once upon a time in the tranquil forest of Fernwood, where the leaves rustled in harmony and the sun filtered through the tall oak trees, two squirrels named Charlie and Larry lived peacefully. They were known far and wide for their charismatic charm and their unusual passion for acorns. Oh, how they adored those tiny, round treasures!

Charlie and Larry were always seen scampering about, gathering their beloved acorns to store away. Their obsession with these little nuts went beyond the ordinary, and they had a secret contest to see who could amass the largest collection. These squirrels wanted a life of comfort, and they knew that their acorn hoard would be their ticket to paradise when winter came.

Every day, they would scurry from tree to tree, their bushy tails wagging and their paws digging into the earth. Each time they stumbled upon an unclaimed acorn on the forest floor, they would eagerly snatch it up, cheering as if they had just won the squirrel lottery.

One day, as Charlie and Larry busily flung acorn after acorn into their respective huts, a wise old owl named Oliver perched on a branch high above, observing their antics. Intrigued by their fervor, he decided to impart some sage advice and flew down to intercept them.

"Charlie! Larry!" Oliver hooted gently, with his eyes gleaming with wisdom. "You two have truly mastered the art of acorn gathering, but have you ever considered the importance of plan-

10

ning for the future?"

Charlie and Larry, caught off guard, stared at the owl with wide eyes, acorns still clutched in their little paws.

"What do you mean, wise old Oliver?" Charlie squeaked. "We've been gathering acorns all day, every day! Isn't that good enough?"

Oliver settled on a branch and, in his calm demeanor, took a moment to ensure he had their undivided attention.

"Ah, my dear squirrels," the owl began, "acorns are undoubtedly valuable, but just like spring turns to winter, the time will come when your hoard will be depleted. You must plan for the day when the acorns won't rain from the sky anymore."

Charlie and Larry exchanged puzzled glances. How could the acorn supply ever dwindle? They had never seen it happen before.

Oliver continued, "You see, squirrels like you live a long life and can face adversity in the form of winter storms, predator attacks, or failed acorn harvests. In such times, it's vital to have a reserve, a savings, if you will. This will guarantee you a comfortable life when you can no longer dart like lightning through the forest."

The squirrel duo absorbed the owl's words, their expressions morphing from confusion to understanding.

"So, what you're saying," Larry mused, "is that if we don't plan for the future when there are plenty of acorns, we might find ourselves in a tough spot when there aren't?"

"Exactly!" Oliver nodded approvingly. "Imagine the peace of mind knowing that your future is secure, just like it is now with your acorn collections. Spend a little less time gathering and start thinking about squirreling away a part of your acorn fortune for the future."

Charlie and Larry, enlightened by the wise old owl's words, put down their acorns and looked at each other thoughtfully. They realized that, while their passion for acorns was well and good, they needed a balance between immediate enjoyment and future security.

The squirrels accepted the challenge themselves, vowing to start saving a portion of their acorn bounty for the day when those acorns became scarce. And as they embarked on their journey to financial security, they encountered a few comical mishaps – mishaps that made them appreciate the value of early planning even more.

From rogue chipmunks eager to snatch their acorns to stealthy raccoons that viewed their stash as a treasure trove, Charlie and Larry faced hilarious obstacles. But throughout it all, they clung to their goal of securing their future, never letting laughter fog their pursuit of a comfortable life.

And so, they continued their days in Fernwood, lightening the forest with their humor and zest for life. Their story became a legend, and their fellow squirrels would often recount the fable of the two wise jokesters who realized the importance of early planning and retired to their cozy nests in comfort, surrounded by their cherished acorns.

Chapter 5: The Ferocious Turtle and the Hasty Hare

Once upon a time, in a bustling forest, there lived a ferocious turtle named Terry and a hasty hare named Harry. Despite their differences, these two creatures were known for their friendly banter, often engaging in bizarre challenges to determine who was the superior animal.

One sunny afternoon, a rumor spread among the animals that a treasure was hidden deep within the forest. This rumor caught the attention of Terry, an ambitious turtle, and Harry, a hare with an undeniable need for instant gratification. The treasure was said to be filled with endless riches, making it the stuff of legends.

Unable to resist the lure of endless wealth, the rivals devised a plan to find the treasure. Though Terry was known for being slow and steady, his patience made him the perfect candidate for a treasure hunt. On the other hand, Harry's lightning-fast speed would be a valuable asset in their pursuit.

The contest was set. The first one to find the treasure and accumulate the most wealth within a month would be declared the victor. Both creatures were given equal sums of money to invest and use as they saw fit.

Harry, with all his hare-like enthusiasm, immediately dashed out of the starting line. He invested heavily in speculative stocks, putting all his eggs in one basket. He was so engrossed in chasing quick gains that he disregarded any financial advice that opposed his rash decisions. Harry's investments soared at first, and

13

he felt like the king of the forest as he saw the imaginary riches magically growing before his eyes.

Meanwhile, Terry, the turtle, took a completely opposite approach. He had always believed in the power of time, patience, and compound interest. Carefully, he divided his money into stocks, bonds, and low-risk investments. Terry understood the importance of diversification and steady growth, rather than chasing fleeting opportunities.

Days turned into weeks, and the forest was filled with laughter and whispers. Harry boasted about his presumed victory, flaunting his newfound riches in front of the other animals. Terry, on the other hand, remained calm and focused on his long-term strategy, content in knowing that time was his most valuable ally.

Then, the unexpected happened – the stock market took a nosedive. Harry's speculative investments crumbled like a weak leaf, leaving him with almost nothing. Panic and stress consumed him, as he realized his hasty approach had led to ruin.

Unbeknownst to Harry, Terry's diversified investments had helped him weather the storm. Sure, he had experienced some loss, but it was small compared to Harry's catastrophic situation. Terry's slow but steady approach had mitigated risks and allowed him to keep his investments afloat.

With only a few days remaining, Harry asked Terry for advice. Bewildered but humbled, Harry acknowledged Terry's wisdom and asked how he managed to survive the market crash with his investments relatively intact.

Terry, with his ever-present smile, explained, "Time, my friend, is the greatest currency when it comes to accumulating wealth. Patience and perseverance may not yield immediate results, but they shield us from the chaos of impulsive actions and give us the ability to ride out market fluctuations."

In the final days of the contest, a remarkable transformation occurred. Terry's investments began to recover, slowly but surely, while Harry realized the importance of time and consistency. Harry, now enlightened, reinvested his remaining money wisely and focused on long-term growth, breaking free from his hasty nature.

When the month came to an end, Terry and Harry met at the treasure site to compare their accumulations. To everyone's surprise, Terry had amassed a wealth that surpassed all expectations, while Harry had managed to recuperate some of his losses, yet still fell far behind.

The forest creatures gathered around in awe of Terry's triumph. But more importantly, they learned a valuable lesson about the power of time, consistency, and wise financial decisions. Terry, the ferocious turtle, had taught them that patience and perseverance are the true keys to financial success.

And so, the forest celebrated Terry's victory – not just for his wealth, but for the wisdom and values he had shared. From that day forward, the forest dwellers collectively decided to honor Terry's legacy by embracing long-term investments, compound interest, and consistent saving habits.

The ferocious turtle had shown them that financial success comes to those who navigate the journey with patience, discipline, and calm under the pressure of instant gratification. And so, their fable remains a joyous reminder that the most valuable and cost-effective asset for accumulating wealth is indeed time itself.

Chapter 6: The Tale of Frugal Freddie and the Mischievous Money Muncher

Once upon a time in the bustling town of Pennypincheria, lived a quirky man named Frugal Freddie. Renowned for his frugality, Freddie was the epitome of thriftiness, always finding a way to make two coins clink together louder than five. His friends and neighbors marveled at his knack for stretching a dollar and sought advice on all matters financial.

One sunny morning, Freddie happened upon a peculiar sight in the local market. There, standing tall on a crate, was a mischievous creature named Monty the Money Muncher. Monty was a sprightly little fellow with eyes that twinkled with mischief. His round torso jiggled with infectious laughter as he regaled the crowd with stories of people squandering their hard-earned cash.

"Listen closely, good people of Pennypincheria!" Monty shouted, his voice booming through the market square. "Have you ever wondered why some folks are always scraping by while others thrive? I'll tell you the secret—it's all about paying yourself first!"

The townsfolk raised their eyebrows, their curiosity piqued. Frugal Freddie, always eager for financial wisdom, edged closer to the crowd, straining to hear Monty's every word.

Monty continued in a playful tone, "You see, ladies and gentlemen, the key to a prosperous future lies in saving before you spend. Paying yourself first means setting aside a portion of your hard-earned money for your future self, before indulging in the finer things in life. Think of it as a treasure chest you build over time, filled with shiny coins that grow and multiply."

The townsfolk nodded thoughtfully, their gazes fixated on Monty's captivating performance.

To demonstrate the consequences of not paying oneself first, Monty whisked away a gullible fellow named Spendthrift Simon. In a twirl of his magical cloak, Monty transported both Freddie and Simon to a fairytale-like room that seemed plucked from a giant piggy bank.

In this whimsical room, piles of gold coins shimmered atop a table, surrounded by enchanting treats – chocolates, cakes, and dazzling trinkets. Seconds later, Simon's eyes widened with delight as he rushed towards the treasures, making a bee-line for the sweets, unable to resist their allure.

Freddie, however, maintained his composure, contemplating the spectacle before him. He approached the table cautiously, intrigued by the glittering coins. Monty chortled with mischief, whispering conspiratorially to Freddie, "Remember, Freddie, in this fable, you represent the prudence of saving!"

Gathering his resolve, Freddie took a deep breath and carefully poured a portion of the coins into a small purse he carried on his belt, while watching Simon happily munch away on all the treats, greedily disregarding the shiny coins.

Just as Freddie secured his purse, a sudden gust of wind swept through the room, snatching the remaining coins from the table. In an instant, the room transformed into a bleak and barren space, devoid of all its previous enchantment. Meanwhile, Simon, too focused on the delights before him, remained oblivious to his diminishing surroundings.

As Monty the Money Muncher vanished, Freddie and Simon were instantly returned to the market square. The crowd gasped in collective realization, their eyes darting between the wiser Freddie and the blissfully ignorant Simon.

Freddie, now clutching his purse tightly, addressed the townspeople with a knowing grin. "The moral of this amusing tale is simple, my friends—a wise person saves for the future, even when surrounded by tempting treats and distractions. By 'paying yourself first,' you ensure a more secure and fulfilling tomorrow, just like the coins in my purse."

The crowd erupted in applause, some even shedding tears of laughter at the absurdity of the situation. Freddie's tale had touched their hearts, sparking a newfound understanding of the importance of prioritizing savings.

And so, dear readers, let us heed Freddie's lesson, for it is not just a fable but a reflection of our own lives. How often do we let the pleasures of today devour our hopes for a brighter future? As Freddie would say, "Give yourself the gift of financial security, and watch your dreams flourish like a money tree."

With that, I encourage you to reflect on your own spending habits. Are you a Spendthrift Simon, or could you use a little more of Frugal Freddie's prudence? Remember, the choice is yours, and your future depends on it.

Chapter 7: The Money Menagerie

Once upon a time in the bustling town of Snaggleton, there lived a mischievous raccoon named Remy, an industrious beaver named Barry, and a wise old owl named Oliver. Each creature had its own unique approach to managing their finances, their contrasting perspectives often led to uproarious events in their friend circle.

Remy, the raccoon, was known throughout Snaggleton for his fascination with shiny objects and his cleverness in getting what he wanted. He had managed to accumulate quite a stash of gold and silver trinkets but was never quite sure what to do with his treasure. So, one day, Remy had a brilliant idea to seek the aid of a financial consultant.

Remy met the ever-confident money-savvy chameleon, Charles, who was renowned for his ability to adapt to various financial landscapes. Posing a puzzle to Charles, Remy pleaded, "Oh, wise Charles! Should I manage my finances independently or hire a financial consultant? What do you think of my shiny stash?"

Charles adjusted his monocle, peered keenly at Remy's collection, and said, "Dear Remy, hiring a financial consultant is like having someone peel your bananas for you. They might get the job done, but did you really need their help? Wouldn't you rather enjoy the satisfaction of peeling your bananas personally?"

Remy pondered Charles' advice but wanted a second opinion. He sought out his hardworking friend, Barry the beaver, known for his practicality and hands-on approach to life.

Finding Barry at his meticulously created dam, Remy posed the same question. "Barry, my utmost buddy, should I entrust my finances to a consultant or tread this path on my own?"

Barry paused, put his paws on his hips, and said, "Why, Remy, a financial consultant is like a whirlpool that promises to take you to a glittering treasure chest but may just leave you gasping for air. It is far better to understand your own finances and chart your own path."

The raccoon grew even more confused. Sensing his turmoil, the ever-wise owl, Oliver, perched himself on a tree branch nearby, observing the furry duo.

With twinkling eyes, Oliver swooped down and joined the conversation. "Remy, my fickle friend, let me spin you a tale that reveals the truth hidden in this financial menagerie. Consider your tasks for the day: collecting your shiny treasures and preserving them for the future. Both Charles and Barry have valid points, but the key lies in balance and knowledge."

Remy blinked. "Balance and knowledge, Oliver? Pray tell!"

"You see, dear Remy," Oliver began, "Be like the chameleon, embracing the positive and adapting to the times by seeking advice from a financial consultant when necessary. However, never rely solely on their expertise. Like the beaver, you must also possess the skills to manage your finances independently, for knowledge is the golden nugget that separates the wise from the misguided."

Remy mulled over Oliver's words, feeling a newfound sense of clarity. He realized the importance of making informed choices and not blindly following any one path. From that day forward, Remy, with a little help from his friends, struck a balance between independent management and occasional financial consultancy.

And so, the animals of Snaggleton never stopped learning and growing, approaching their financial adventures with a healthy dose of wit and wisdom. They understood that the true treasures of life were not just shiny objects, but also the ability to make informed financial decisions to secure their future.

Moral of the story: Balancing independence and knowledge brings forth financial wisdom, much like a perfectly balanced diet nourishes the body and soul. So, dear readers, may you heed the words of our furry friends and tread the path of informed financial decisions, enriching your lives along the way.

Chapter 8: The Tragic Demise of the 3-Legged Stool: A Comedy of Errors

Once upon a time, in a land far, far, a wise old salesman touted the virtues of a miraculous invention called the "3-legged stool" for retirement planning. It was said that this ingenious contraption, composed of Social Security, pension plans, and personal savings, would support even the wobbliest of potential retirees. Oh, how the people rejoiced at the thought of a blissful retirement atop this mythological masterpiece! Little did they know the comedy of errors that lay ahead.

As the years went by, the cracks in the three-legged stool grew wider, and its once-sturdy foundation began to crumble. It became increasingly apparent that relying on this antiquated relic was about as wise as relying on an asthmatic tortoise to sprint a marathon.

The first leg of this absurd stool, Social Security, seemed destined to pull the rug out from under our hopes of a golden retirement. It's like relying on a spoon to dethrone King Kong or attempting to quench a forest fire with a water pistol. We've all seen the headlines, my friends: "Social Security Running Out of Money," "Baby Boomers Blues: Will There Be Anything Left for Me?" If we were to choose a metaphor, it would be a majestic castle built on quicksand, slowly sinking into the abyss of unfunded liabilities.

Now, let us cringe as we shift our gaze to the second leg of this ill-fated stool: pension plans. Oh, how the mighty have fallen! Pension plans, once the holy grail of retirement security, morphed into ticking time bombs of underfunded misery. Picture this, if you will: an aspiring retiree handing their pension fund manager a lottery ticket as their sole retirement savings strategy. That would be like trusting a circus clown to perform open-heart surgery while riding a unicycle. Spoiler alert: it's not going to end well.

But fear not, for the third leg of this tragicomic stool promises us salvation, right? Alas, personal savings have sadly become the Rodney Dangerfield of retirement planning – they get no respect! With the average American juggling bills, student loans, and the ever-present temptation of online shopping, saving for retirement can feel like trying to give a cat a bubble bath. It's an exercise in futility, my friends.

Let's add a splash of real-life absurdity to this comedy of errors, shall we? Picture an elderly couple, romantically embracing in their gold-plated Jacuzzi, surrounded by stacks of unpaid bills. Just as they sip champagne from crystal glasses, their doorbell ominously rings, announcing a visit from the repo man. The reason for this cruel interruption? They had mistakenly relied on the three-legged stool, trusting it would shield them from financial ruin. But alas, this poor couple mistakenly funded their extravagant lifestyle with Monopoly money and used their life savings to make paper airplanes for their grandchildren.

In our modern world, clinging to this once-viable three-legged stool is like bringing a rubber chicken to a swordfight. It's time to toss the stool aside and embrace a more sensible approach to retirement planning. Picture a futuristic jetpack of financial freedom, propelled by a diversified investment portfolio, multiple streams of income, and the power of compound interest. Now that's something you can strut your stuff on!

As we bid farewell to the tragic demise of the three-legged stool, let us recognize the importance of adapting to the ever-changing landscape of retirement planning. Let us embrace modern strategies and remember that in today's world, relying on a three-legged stool is about as helpful as putting a Band-Aid on a bullet wound.

So, my dear readers, embrace laughter, learn from the follies of the past, and build a retirement plan that will support you like the grandest trapeze artist, flying high above the circus of financial insecurity. Safe travels, my friends!

Chapter 9: The Monkey Business of Compound Interest

Once upon a time in a land ruled by monkeys (we promise this isn't a joke, just a whimsical setting), a monkey named Max stumbled upon a mysterious banana tree. But this wasn't any ordinary banana tree, oh no! This tree magically grew one banana every day.

Max, being a savvy monkey, knew that bananas were a treasure beyond measure and couldn't wait to share his newfound wealth. However, he also knew he had to find a way to ensure he would never run out of bananas. That's when he discovered the astonishing power of compound interest.

Now compound interest sounds like a fancy financial term that'll have you scratching your head, but it's quite simple when you think about it. It's like when your friend asks you to borrow some money but then has to pay you back not only that initial amount but also a little extra for your troubles. It's like getting interest on interest. Sounds pretty neat, right?

Max decided to invest five of his bananas into a new business venture: a tropical smoothie stand. Customers flocked to Max's stand, and soon he was making a profit of one banana every day. And this is where the magic of compound interest comes into play.

You see, Max didn't spend all his profits on bananas to munch on. Instead, he started investing them back into his business, buying more equipment, and even hiring a few friends to help. With more smoothies being made, customers were getting hooked on Max's delicious concoctions, and his profit grew to two bananas each day.

Now, this is where compound interest starts showing its surprising power. Max thought to himself, "I can save one banana a day while still enjoying my daily banana smoothie, and invest the rest to fund my dream of a banana-napping island retirement home!"

Max knew that the longer he kept this investment game going, the greater his wealth would become, thanks to the magic of compound interest. So off he went to an island, sipping his refreshing, fruity smoothie, and enjoying the sun whilst his banana-napping island retirement home slowly took shape (monkeys need a place to rest their furry bums too).

While Max was happily sunbathing, his investments kept multiplying, thanks to compound interest. By reinvesting his daily profit and letting the money grow, he was swimming in bananas (not literally, that would be weird and messy).

Back in his monkey world, everyone soon realized the astonishing power of compound interest. They said, "If Max could turn five bananas into an island paradise and a lifetime supply of fruity drinks, what could we achieve if we joined the bandwagon?"

And so, banana trees sprouted everywhere (also not weird, remember, monkey world!). Soon, all the monkeys were building their businesses and optimizing their returns by reinvesting their profits. The monkey economy boomed, and it was all thanks to compound interest.

So the moral of this banana-filled story is this: while compound interest may seem like a distant and dull concept, it can turn a small investment into a substantial pile of fruit. Whether you're saving for retirement, a dream vacation, or your very own banana-napping island, remember that investing your money wisely with compound interest can make your dreams a reality.

And just like Max, may you all be blessed with plenty of bananas and the flourishing wealth that comes with it. But beware, no monkeying around with compound interest! Trust us, monkey business is only fun up to a point.

Now go forth, my fellow readers, armed with the knowledge of compound interest, and conquer the financial jungles with your newfound understanding. And always remember, the power of compound interest is truly bananas!

James "Jimmy" Glascott, a true champion of the world of finance, has been making waves in the financial services and insurance industry for over two decades. With an impressive 22 years of expertise under his belt, Jimmy has cemented his position as a seasoned professional in his field. However, it is his unwavering passion for promoting financial literacy that truly sets him apart.

Jimmy's journey is a testament to his commitment to helping others navigate the complex world of finance. In a nightmarish turn of events 22 years ago, he found himself losing a staggering 50% of his hard-earned retirement savings. This devastating blow catalyzed Jimmy to embark on a mission to educate others and prevent them from falling prey to similar financial calamities.

Driven by a desire to empower individuals and promote financial literacy, Jimmy has dedicated his life to sharing his knowledge and expertise. His notable book, "Financial Fun: Separating Myths from Truth in Hilarious Fables," captures his unique approach to financial education. Through intriguing and often comical fables, Jimmy offers readers a fresh and engaging perspective on the otherwise daunting subject of finance.

With a descriptive and engaging tone, Jimmy draws readers in, making the ideas and concepts relatable and accessible. By skillfully blending humor and wisdom, he effortlessly demonstrates the power of storytelling as a means of imparting financial knowledge. "Financial Fun" is not just another dry textbook on finance; it is an invitation to embrace the intricacies of the financial realm with a newfound curiosity and sense of adventure. Jimmy's contributions to the field of finance extend far beyond the pages of his book. Through speaking engagements, workshops, and one-on-one consultations, he has positively impacted the lives of countless individuals. He has tirelessly sought to equip people with the tools and knowledge they need to take control of their financial futures, transforming their outlooks and empowering them to make informed decisions.

It is Jimmy's genuine passion for promoting financial literacy, coupled with his own harrowing experience, that sets him apart as an expert in his field. His ability to demystify complex financial concepts and impart knowledge with humor and relatability makes him a valued and respected figure in the world of finance.

So, as you embark on your financial journey, let Jimmy be your guide. Whether you're a seasoned investor or just beginning your foray into finance, Jimmy's insights are sure to captivate and enlighten you. Once you delve into the world of "Financial Fun: Separating Myths from Truth in Hilarious Fables," you'll gain not only valuable knowledge but also a newfound enthusiasm for navigating the ever-changing landscape of personal finance. Prepare to be inspired and enlightened by the remarkable contributions of Jimmy Glascott – a true advocate for financial literacy.

"Financial Fun: Separating Myth from Truth in Hilarious Fables" is a must-read for anyone seeking to unravel the mysteries of personal finance with a side-splitting twist. This one-of-a-kind book offers a rare blend of humor and expertise, enlightening readers through uproarious stories and anecdotes that debunk financial misconceptions.

Are you tired of dry, complicated financial advice? Look no further! "Financial Fun" will have you laughing out loud while effortlessly gaining valuable knowledge about money matters. From the moment you open this book, you'll be whisked away on a journey filled with wit and wisdom that will transform your understanding of personal finance.

Imagine learning about the pitfalls of credit card debt through the hilarious tale of a daring gambler who discovers the hard way that "easy money" comes at a steep cost. Or, dive into the world of investing with a story that cunningly unmasks the myth that only the wealthy can grow their wealth, revealing that anyone with enough knowledge and a dash of strategic thinking can thrive in the market.

"Financial Fun" tackles a wide range of financial topics, from budgeting and savings to retirement planning and beyond, debunking common myths along the way. Each fable is carefully crafted to entertain and educate, making the learning experience engaging and enjoyable.

Prepare to be captivated by the author's masterful storytelling, as they expertly weave together humor and valuable insights. As you delve into each colorful fable, you'll find yourself hooked, eagerly turning the pages to discover how the protagonist navigates their financial challenges.

Whether you're a finance novice or an experienced money-handler, "Financial Fun" offers something for everyone. It's a book that teaches without lecturing, enlightens without overwhelming, and entertains without sacrificing substance.

So, if you're ready to laugh, learn, and separate fact from fiction in the world of finance, grab a copy of "Financial Fun: Separating Myth from Truth in Hilarious Fables" today. Get ready for an unforgettable reading experience that will leave you both entertained and armed with newfound financial wisdom.

Chapter 10: The Tale of Penny the Piggy-bank

Once upon a time, in the bustling town of Moneyville, there lived a merry piggybank called Penny. Penny was just like any other piggybank, with a jolly round body and a cheerful smile painted on her face. She was adored by all the townspeople and had a knack for collecting shiny coins.

Now, Penny had a friend named Sammy, the wise old owl. Sammy was known for his vast knowledge of all things related to money, and Penny was always keen to hear his stories. One sunny afternoon, as Penny sat on the windowsill, Sammy gently landed beside her.

"Penny my dear, I have a tale to share with you," said Sammy, his eyes twinkling. "It's about the fascinating world of compound interest."

Penny's little piggy ears perked up with curiosity. "Oh please, Sammy! Tell me more!"

Sammy cleared his throat and began spinning a whimsical tale. "Once upon a time, there were two wealthy neighbors named Benjamin and Walter. Both had saved a hefty sum of money, but their approach to growing their wealth was quite different."

Penny's eyes gleamed with excitement. "Do tell! I love a good story."

"Well," continued Sammy, adjusting his spectacles, "Benjamin was a simple man, so he deposited his hard-earned money into a savings account that offered him a fixed annual interest rate. Let's call it Simple Savings Bank."

Penny nodded, hanging on to every word. "And what about Walter?"

"Walter, my dear Penny, was a smart squirrel who believed in the magic of compound interest. He decided to invest his money in a special tree, where his savings would grow over time. It was called the Magical Money Tree."

"Oh, how intriguing!" Penny exclaimed, her hooves twitching with excitement.

"Now, Penny, listen closely," Sammy said, leaning closer to her. "One day, they both made a deposit of $100 into their respective accounts. Benjamin's account offered an annual simple interest rate of 5%, whereas Walter's Magical Money Tree promised a compound interest rate of 5% as well."

Penny's eyes widened with expectation. "What happened next, Sammy?"

"Time passed, my dear, and the simplicity of Benjamin's savings account became apparent. At the end of the first year, he earned an interest of $5," Sammy paused.

"Oh, that's nice!" Penny chuckled.

"But Penny, it's time for Walter's grand reveal!" Sammy beamed. "Thanks to the power of compound interest, Walter's tree blossomed even more. At the end of the first year, Walter's Magical Money Tree grew by $5, just like Benjamin's savings account.

However, here's where it gets interesting – instead of leaving that $5 for himself, Walter reinvested it back into the tree."

Penny's eyes widened in surprise. "He did what?!"

"Yes, dear Penny! Each year, Walter continued to reinvest his earnings into the Magical Money Tree, letting compound interest work its magic. As a result, his money started growing like wildfire!"

Penny gasped, her mind spinning with wonder. "So... how much did Walter eventually end up with, Sammy?"

"Ah, my dear Penny, that's the best part of the tale!" Sammy said, with a mischievous twinkle in his eyes. "After 20 years, Benjamin's simple interest account grew to a total of $200."

Penny's jaw dropped. "Just $200?"

"But wait for it, my friend," Sammy said, his voice filled with excitement. "Walter's Magical Money Tree, fueled by the power of compound interest, flourished and grew to a staggering $265!"

Penny's eyes almost popped out of her head. "Sammy, that's incredible!"

Sammy chuckled, ruffling his feathers. "Indeed, Penny! Compound interest has the power to multiply your money, as the interest earned each year accumulates and helps your savings grow at an increasing rate over time."

Penny sat in awe of the tale she had just heard, her smile stretching from one end of her face to the other. From that day forward, Penny became a beacon of wisdom in Moneyville, teaching all her fellow piggybanks about the incredible benefits of compound interest.

And so, dear reader, the delightful tale of Penny the Piggybank ends with a valuable lesson: compound interest can turn even the humblest savings into a treasure trove of abundance.

Chapter 11: The Adventures of Penny the Prodigal Pigeon

Once upon a time, in the buzzing city of Featherington, there was a flock of pigeons living happily near the Grand Hotel on Diamond Street. Among them, there was a young and curious pigeon named Penny. Penny had a penchant for shiny things and a resilient spirit that often led her to exciting (and sometimes dangerous) escapades.

One bright morning, Penny found herself perched on a branch next to her older and wiser friend, Perry the Pigeon. Perry, being known for his financial acumen, often shared his wisdom with Penny.

"Penny, my dear, have you ever heard of the #1 rule of money?" Perry asked, his voice filled with an air of importance.

Penny, ever the eager beak, replied, "Oh, pray tell, Perry! What could it be?"

A twinkle came to Perry's eyes as he gracefully adjusted his feathers and began his fable:

"Once, in the land of Featherington, there lived a flamboyant magpie named Magnus. Magnus was known far and wide for his ostentatious lifestyle and extravagant manner of speech. The entire city marveled at his shiny collection, envy filling their hearts as they gazed upon his glittering treasures."

Penny, her wings flapping with delight, interrupted Perry. "Oh, Perry! Tell me more about this marvelous magpie."
36

But Perry, ever the maestro of suspense, hushed Penny with a silent wing wave.

"Now, Penny, one day, Magnus grew tired of his possession-filled nest and wanted to explore the world beyond Featherington. But he had a small problem. Magnus had no notion of the #1 rule of money: 'Do not lose money.'"

Penny gasped, her feathers ruffling with anticipation. "Poor Magnus! What did he do?"

Perry continued, his voice filled with caution. "Magnus gathered his riches, filled them into a precious golden pouch, and set off on his journey, his eyes filled with anticipation. However, his irresistible desire for shiny things proved too strong."

As Penny leaned in closer, Perry's voice dropped to a whisper. "A mischievous raven, known as Roderick, spotted Magnus from atop a tall oak tree. Roderick had a reputation for trickery and deceit, and he noticed that Magnus's pouch seemed vulnerable."

"Oh no!" Penny exclaimed, her eyes wide with concern. "Tell me, Perry, what happened next?"

"Well," Perry said solemnly, "Roderick couldn't resist the allure of Magnus's pouch. So, with great cunning, he devised a plan to distract the magpie."

Perry's wings fluttered with excitement, imitating Roderick's cunning exploits. "Roderick began to caw loudly, flying around Magnus in a whirlwind of chaos. Poor Magnus tried to swat him away, but the cunning raven succeeded. As Magnus's attention was diverted, Roderick snatched the golden pouch and flew off into the distance."

Penny's beak dropped open, her feathers fluffed with disbelief. "Oh no! Did Magnus ever find his lost treasure?"

"Well, my dear," Perry said, a note of wisdom in his voice, "Magnus spent the rest of his days searching for his beloved pouch, but he never found it. He had learned a costly lesson about the importance of not losing money."

Penny looked thoughtful, her eyes glimmering with newfound understanding. "So, Perry, that's why the #1 rule of money is 'Do not lose money.' Losing money can be as painful as losing a shiny pouch."

Perry nodded with a beakful of pride. "Indeed, young Penny. Remember, it's not about how much you have, but rather how you protect what you possess."

And so, in the land of Featherington, Penny the Prodigal Pigeon learned a valuable lesson from Perry the Wise. From that day forward, she flew a little more cautiously, always keeping an eye on her shiny findings, and never forgetting the #1 rule of money: "Do not lose money."

In the end, dear reader, the moral remains clear: regardless of how much you have, taking care of what you possess is a treasure in itself.

Chapter 12: The Wise Tortoise and the Mischievous Hare

Once upon a time in the magical land of Numeria, there lived a wise old tortoise named Terry and a mischievous hare called Harry. Despite their differences, they were great friends and loved to explore new financial concepts together.

One sunny afternoon, Terry and Harry were lounging under an enormous oak tree, when Harry, in his usual impulsive manner, exclaimed, "Hey Terry, have you heard about this rule of 72 thing everyone's talking about? I can't wrap my fluffy head around it!"

Terry, being the wise tortoise that he was, replied with a chuckle, "Ah, Harry, my friend, let me tell you a tale that will unravel the mystery of the rule of 72."

As Terry spoke, the animals gathered around, intrigued by the prospect of a fable about finance. Even a chipmunk named Charlie scuttled closer to listen, eager for some financial wisdom.

"Once upon a time," Terry began, "there lived a farmer named Fredrick, who had a field filled with magical carrots. These carrots multiplied as no other crop could. Fredrick was a clever farmer and realized he could sell these multiplying carrots and make a fortune. So, he decided to plant them all together and waited for them to grow."

The forest animals giggled, imagining a field of carrots multiplying like rabbits (as they are known to do). They could hardly contain their laughter.

39

"Now, Harry," Terry continued, "let's say Fredrick's magical carrots multiplied by 100 every year. That means, at the end of the first year, he would have 100 carrots. At the end of the second year, he'd have 10,000 carrots. And so on."

Harry's eyes widened with amazement. "Wow, Terry, that's some serious multiplication power!"

Terry nodded, savoring the moment as he saw the concept sinking in. Then, he continued, "Now, the rule of 72 tells us how long it will take for Fredrick's investment to double. All you have to do is divide 72 by the annual growth rate."

Harry, eager to be involved, quickly calculated, "So, if the magical carrots multiply by 100 every year, I divide 100 by 72 and get 1.38 years?"

The animals burst into laughter, rolling on the ground, tears streaming from their eyes at Harry's hilarious misunderstanding.

Terry, still chuckling, replied, "Oh, Harry, my friend, we must remember to convert the growth rate into a percentage. So, in this case, 100% growth rate gives us 72/100 = 0.72 years to double."

Harry blushed in embarrassment, realizing his math faux pas. But Terry, being a good friend, continued, "Think of the rule of 72 as a quick way to estimate how long it will take for an investment to double. If Fredrick wanted to have 200 magical carrots, he'd divide 72 by 200 (the desired doubling rate), yielding 0.36 years, or roughly four months."

The forest animals marveled at Terry's wisdom, their laughter fading into appreciation. They could finally see the usefulness of this magical math concept.

Charlie, the chipmunk, spoke up eagerly, "So, an investor could use the rule of 72 to estimate how many years it would take to double their money?"

Terry nodded approvingly. "Exactly, Charlie! It's a handy tool to compare different investments. For example, if a bank offers an interest rate of 3%, you can use the rule of 72 to estimate that it'll take around 24 years to double your money. But if a unicorn investment manager promises a 12% return, it'll take just six years."

As the animals digested this newfound financial knowledge, a subtle but satisfying aroma wafted through the air – the smell of freshly baked carrot muffins. Fredrick the farmer had turned his magical carrots into sweet treats for everyone in the forest.

And so, the wise tortoise Terry, the mischievous hare Harry, and all their animal friends feasted on carrot muffins and basked in the delight of both financial wit and the magic of their friendship, forever understanding the rule of 72.

And as they ventured into the sunset, there arose a whispered chorus among them: "Divide 72 by the growth rate, and thou shall grasp the secrets of compound interest!"

The end... for now.

Chapter 13: The Rule of 100 - The Owl and The Squirrel Gambit

Once upon a time in the whimsical world of Woodlandia, there lived two animal friends who were always up to some mischief: Oliver the Wise Owl and Sammie the Scheming Squirrel. These two characters had a knack for finding themselves in the most peculiar predicaments, and this time was no exception.

One sunny afternoon, as leaves whispered secrets and the flowers bloomed happily, Oliver and Sammie found themselves deep in a conversation about retirement planning. Oliver, being the wise old owl, was regaling Sammie with the latest financial advice he had learned.

"Ah, Sammie," Oliver declared, perched atop a sturdy branch. "In the realm of retirement planning, there exists a rule known as the Rule of 100. It's a handy guideline to help you determine the right balance between risk and safety."

Sammie, his tiny paws clutching a chewed-up acorn, looked perplexed. "Uh, Oliver, what on earth is the Rule of 100? And why should I care about it?"

Oliver chuckled softly, his eyes twinkling in amusement. "Well, Sammie, let me explain. You see, the Rule of 100 suggests that you should subtract your age from 100. The resulting number will represent the percentage of your total portfolio that you should invest in stocks or other potentially higher-risk assets."

Sammie's eyes widened in astonishment. "Wow, Oliver, that sounds fascinating! But does it really work? Sounds too good to be true."

Oliver adjusted his glasses and replied, "Ah, my dear Sammie, that's where it gets interesting. The rule provides a broad framework, but it doesn't take into account individual financial situations and risk tolerance."

Unbeknownst to them, a mischievous wind whispered their conversation to Gabby the Great Generalist, a squirrel renowned for her ability to uncover financial secrets. Gabby was always on the lookout for an opportunity, and the Rule of 100 captured her undivided attention.

"Wise owls and scheming squirrels, eh? This might be a tale worth telling!" she mused, her fluffy tail swaying with excitement.

Gabby hatched a plan to set a challenge for Oliver and Sammie. She snuck into their conversation and posed a question in her most mysterious voice, "Oh, honored friends, would you dare to embark on a grand competition to test the very limits of the Rule of 100?"

Oliver and Sammie exchanged curious glances. Their adventurous spirits couldn't resist the intrigue of Gabby's challenge.

"Alright, Gabby," Sammie chattered eagerly, "count us in! What do we have to do?"

Gabby leaned forward, her beady eyes sparkling. "You have to invest each other's savings according to the Rule of 100 for an entire year, and the one who earns higher returns shall be deemed the true master of the Rule!"

Oliver and Sammie gulped nervously. The thought of managing each other's life savings in pursuit of honor and glory sent shivers down their spines. Yet, who could resist the lure of a thrilling challenge?

Over the next year, the story of Oliver and Sammie's unconventional investment experiment spread like wildfire through the enchanted forest of Woodlandia. Ferrets huddled in dark corners to discuss it, rabbits organized betting pools, while wise old badgers watched from afar, amused.

Oliver, with his vast knowledge and careful calculations, diligently followed the Rule of 100, meticulously assigning Sammie's savings to low-risk assets befitting her age, while Sammie, notorious for her love of excitement, recklessly plunged Oliver's fortune into high-yield but volatile investments.

The amusing escapades of Oliver and Sammie brought forth a series of comedic situations. From Oliver's frustration at watching his portfolio gain slow but steady growth to Sammie's wild nights crunching numbers and fretting over each stock market twist, it was a contest of wit, luck, and sheer comedic chaos.

Through the ups and downs, the wise owl and the scheming squirrel learned valuable lessons about the Rule of 100. They discovered that while the rule offered a useful starting point, it wasn't foolproof and couldn't replace personalized financial planning. It hinted at the importance of considering one's risk tolerance, financial goals, and lifestyle, rather than blindly adhering to a generic rule.

As the year drew to a close, both Oliver and Sammie anxiously awaited the final results of their daring competition. With a grand gathering of Woodlandia's finest critters, Gabby the Great Generalist declared the winner.

"In a stunning turn of events, dear friends, Oliver's careful adherence to the Rule of 100 has triumphed!" Gabby announced, her voice echoing through the enchanted forest.

Oliver and Sammie exchanged relieved glances. The experience had taught them that while the Rule of 100 provides a useful framework, blindly sticking to it without considering personal circumstances could lead to unexpected consequences.

Woodlandia celebrated Oliver's victory with a grand feast, and the story of their escapades lingered in the hearts and minds of Woodlandia's critters for generations to come. The tale of the owl and the squirrel reminded them to approach retirement planning with a careful mix of diligence, flexibility, and a touch of animal mischief.

And so, dear reader, remember Oliver and Sammie's escapades as you navigate the treacherous yet fascinating world of retirement planning. Let their tale be a guide to reminding you of the importance of thoughtful financial strategies, adaptability to your unique circumstances, and the risks that lie in blindly adhering to any rule, no matter how whimsically intriguing.

Chapter 14: The Fatigued Rule: Fable of Financial Planning

Once upon a time the land of Certainty, there lived a retired tortoise named Timothy. He had followed the traditional 4% rule, which suggested he could withdraw 4% from his savings each year without worrying about running out of money. However, poor Timothy found himself feeling anything but certain.

One sunny morning, as Timothy strolled through the town square, he stumbled upon his old friend, a wise and witty rabbit named Robert. Intrigued by his friend's gloomy expression, Robert hopped over and said, "Good day, Timothy. Why do you look so weary? Retirement is meant to be a time of leisure and relaxation!"

Timothy let out a sigh. "Oh, Robert, my friend, retirement is far from relaxing when you're bound by the Fatigued Rule!"

Robert raised an eyebrow, perplexed. "The Fatigued Rule? Pray tell, dear Timothy, what is this Fatigued Rule you speak of?"

Timothy leaned in, his voice filled with both fatigue and frustration. "Well, my wisecracking friend, it's the widely championed 4% rule. Supposedly, if you limit your annual withdrawals to 4% of your retirement savings, it will last you a lifetime. But let me tell you, it's been nothing short of exhausting!"

Robert chuckled, thinking Timothy was being overly dramatic. "Exhausting? Why, Timothy, it is the golden rule of retirement planning! What could possibly be so tiresome about it?"

Timothy glanced around, making sure no one was within earshot before whispering, "Robert, my friend, the Fatigued Rule ignores real-life fluctuations and risks. It assumes a linear and stable return on investments, something we all know rarely exists."

Robert's eyes widened, realization dawning on him. "Ah, so you're tired of constantly worrying if your investment returns will cooperate!"

Timothy nodded wearily. "Precisely! Take this year, for example. My investments took a nosedive due to market volatility, and my 4% withdrawal became much too large a chunk of my remaining savings. The Fatigued Rule doesn't account for such unexpected setbacks!"

Robert scratched his fur, contemplating Timothy's dilemma. "I see your point, my friend. The Fatigued Rule indeed appears to be a bit too rigid. What alternatives have you explored?"

Timothy's eyes sparkled with newfound determination. "I've discovered that flexible withdrawal strategies, like the dynamic spending approach, offer a better chance for retirees to navigate unpredictable market conditions. By adjusting our withdrawals in response to market performance, we can preserve our savings and enjoy a more financially secure retirement."

Robert nodded, impressed by Timothy's newfound wisdom. "Aha! The Fatigued Rule may have tired you, but you rose above it, my friend. You've grasped the essence of financial planning – adaptability!"

As Timothy and Robert continued their lively conversation,

word spread throughout the town of Timothy's newfound financial wisdom. Retirees emerged from their cocoons of certainty, eager to embrace alternative approaches to retirement planning.

And so, dear readers, we learn an essential lesson from Timothy's adventures – traditional rules may have their place, but they should never blind us to the possibilities beyond. By blending humor and satire with insightful analysis, we discover the true treasures of financial planning strategies.

So, go forth, my friends, and let the Fatigued Rule rest, as you open your minds to flexible, adaptable retirement strategies. May you find not only financial freedom but also the joy of writing your own fable in the treasury of retirement planning.

The end.

Chapter 15: The Diversification Dilemma
The Woodpecker's Wisdom

Once upon a time, in a quaint forest full of wise creatures, there lived a diligent little woodpecker named Woody. Woody was known for his sharp beak and his keen eye for spotting hidden treasures. Every day, he would tirelessly peck at trees, searching for delicious insects and tasty grubs. Along with his fellow bird friends, Woody lived a simple life, constantly striving to secure their future.

One sunny day, Woody overheard some squirrels chattering away about their retirement plans. They gleefully shared tales of how they had squirreled away nuts in various locations, so they'd always have enough for the future. Woody, intrigued by their strategy, approached them to learn more.

"Hello, wise squirrels! I couldn't help but overhear your retirement plans. It seems you rely on diversification to secure your future. But is that the best way to prepare for retirement?"

The squirrels paused, exchanging curious glances before one of them replied, "Ah, dear Woody, diversification is the key to a secure retirement. By spreading our nuts across different places, we minimize the risk of losing everything should a predator or an unfortunate event befall one location. It's important to not put all our nuts in one tree, you know?"

Woody pondered their advice, but it didn't quite sit right with him. Determined to explore this concept further, he set off on a journey across the forest in search of answers.

His first stop was the bustling beehive, known for its industrious inhabitants. Woody recounted his conversation with the squirrels to the bees, who decided to share their wisdom.

"Woodpecker, diversification is like pollen to flowers. We cannot rely on a single source of pollen or a single type of flower for our survival. By visiting different flowers, we ensure variety in our diet and enhance the resilience of our hive. Diversification is simply nature's way of hedging against unforeseen events."

Despite the bees' assurances, Woody's feathers ruffled with skepticism. He wasn't satisfied with these limited perspectives. Continuing on, he stumbled into the lair of a wise old fox named Felix. Surely, the fox would have a different take on diversification.

"Ah, Woody, my curious friend! Come and sit by the fire," Felix beckoned. "Diversification is indeed a useful principle, but one must be cautious. Those who blindly rely on diversification may lose sight of the opportunities that come from specialization. By focusing on honing our unique strengths, we can achieve mastery and reap the rewards that come with it."

Woody listened intently to Felix's words, realizing that diversification is not the cure-all solution it is often presumed to be. Determined to unravel this mystery, he ventured deeper into the forest, searching for more wisdom.

Finally, he found himself before the wise owl, Oliver, perched atop the highest branch of a towering tree. With ancient wisdom shining in his eyes, Oliver shared his perspective.

"Woodpecker, diversification is wise, but it is not without its flaws. While it spreads risk, it can also dampen returns. When resources are spread too thin, they cannot fully flourish. It's a delicate balance, my friend. Too much diversification and you may find yourself in mediocrity, but too little and you risk catastrophe."

Woody's journey came to an end as he sat in deep contemplation. All the wisdom he had gathered painted a complex picture of diversification. It was neither a foolproof strategy nor a frivolous myth, but rather a tool that required delicate handling.

Returning to his fellow birds, Woody shared his findings, urging them to reflect before blindly accepting widely held beliefs. The birds discussed and debated, each realizing the need to evaluate diversification on an individual basis. Some concluded that moderate diversification was prudent, striking a balance between specialization and spreading risk.

And so, Woody left his fellow birds with a newfound wisdom and a refreshed perspective. From that day forward, they together soared through the forest, no longer blinded by the deception of a single, magical solution. The lesson they learned, my friends, is that diversification must be carefully considered and tailored to one's unique circumstances.

Remember, as you embark on your retirement journey, be an avid student of wisdom like Woody. Explore the complexities, question the assumptions, and seek that balanced path. Only then can you truly retire happily ever after.

Chapter 16: The Wise Ant and the Foolish Grasshopper: Unveiling the Essence of Risk Mitigation in Retirement Planning

Once upon a time, in a lush meadow filled with vibrant flowers and bustling insects, two creatures named Archie the Ant and Gilbert the Grasshopper were engaged in a spirited conversation. Archie, with his wise old eyes and calculative demeanor, represented prudence and forethought in all things financial. Gilbert, a carefree and jovial soul, sought laughter and merriment, much to the annoyance of Archie.

One sunny afternoon, as the scent of wildflowers wafted through the air, the topic of retirement planning emerged between the unlikely pair. Archie, ever the responsible advisor, urged Gilbert to consider the importance of risk mitigation strategies for their golden years.

"Dear Gilbert," Archie began, adjusting his spectacles, "retirement is like a grand feast. If you do not plan and prepare wisely, you may end up feasting on bread crumbs instead of seasoned delicacies."

Gilbert, idly hopping from flower to flower, chuckled at Archie's words. "Oh dear Archie," he chimed, "why worry about the future when we have such a beautiful present? Life's too short to spend it all working and worrying about what's to come."

Archie sighed, realizing he had quite a challenge on his six tiny legs. Determined to impart his wisdom, he conjured a tale that would captivate even Gilbert's carefree spirit.

52

"Once, in a faraway ant kingdom, there lived a wise ant named Augusta and a foolish grasshopper named Gideon," Archie began, capturing Gilbert's attention.

Augusta, much like Archie himself, was a diligent planner, constantly preparing for the changes and challenges that lay ahead. Gideon, on the other hand, hopped through life without a care, singing and fiddling away his days, much to the annoyance of Augusta.

One particularly cold winter, as the grasshopper shivered and sought refuge in Augusta's well-stocked anthill, Gideon realized his squandered opportunities. This misfortune led to a heartfelt conversation between the two unlikely companions.

"Augusta," Gideon whispered, his wings drooping, "I now realize the importance of your prudence. I've danced through life without considering the consequences, and now I find myself in trouble. Please, teach me the ways of retirement planning before it's too late."

Augusta, with compassion in her eyes, shared her knowledge with Gideon. "Retirement, my dear friend, is not about extinguishing the joys of life. It is about balancing prudence and enjoyment. Just as we store food for the winter, we must store financial wisdom for our golden years."

With a series of amusing anecdotes and clever tips, Augusta guided Gideon towards understanding the essence of risk mitigation. She emphasized the need to diversify investments, cautiously explore high-risk endeavors, and diligently save for emergencies.

As their story unfolded, Archie noticed Gilbert's eyes growing wider and his carefree demeanor slowly transforming into thoughtful contemplation.

"Dear Gilbert," Archie continued, leaning closer, "the moral of the tale is this: enjoying life today should not come at the expense of our future happiness. By embracing risk mitigation strategies, we can prudently navigate through retirement, savoring the fruits of our labor while safeguarding against unforeseen challenges."

Gilbert, now fully engrossed in the wisdom of Archie's tale, nodded his head in understanding. "Archie," he confessed with gratitude, "I shall forever treasure the balance between joy and prudence as I journey towards retirement. After all, life is meant to be savored, just like a delectable wildflower on a warm summer's day."

And so, as the sun set over the enchanting meadow, Archie and Gilbert continued their enlightening conversation, each bringing a unique perspective to the dance of life and the importance of risk mitigation in retirement planning. Together, they traversed the meadow, spreading their witty wisdom to all who would listen, ensuring a harmonious retirement for every creature that roamed the land.

And thus, the timeless lessons of financial wisdom echoed from the meadows, reminding one and all to embrace both prudence and pleasure and dance through life with a balanced heart and filled coffers.

That, dear reader, is the whimsical tale of The Wise Ant and the

Foolish Grasshopper: Unveiling the Essence of Risk Mitigation in Retirement Planning. Remember it well, for in its core lies the secret to a fulfilling and worry-free retirement.

Chapter 17: The Tax Turtle and the Clever Chameleon

Once upon a time, in the bustling town of Financia, there lived an old tax turtle named Terrence. Terrence was known for his vast knowledge of financial matters, especially when it came to retirement planning. He had seen it all – the ups and downs of the markets, the rise and fall of fortunes, and of course, the ins and outs of taxes.

One sunny day, as Terrence was making his way to the local pond, he noticed a group of animals huddled together, whispering and giggling. Curiosity piqued, the wise turtle slowly approached, intrigued by what seemed to be a tremendous secret.

"What's all the commotion about?" Terrence asked, his wise eyes twinkling.

The animals quickly quieted down, and one by one, they turned towards Terrence, as if they had been waiting for his arrival. It turned out, my friend, that they were indeed waiting for him. News of his financial wisdom had spread through the animal kingdom, and they were now seeking his help with their retirement plans.

Among them was a clever chameleon named Charlie, who was known for his vibrant personality and his uncanny ability to blend into any situation. Charlie approached Terrence with a wry smile and said, "Ah, Terrence, my dear turtle friend, I'm in desperate need of some financial advice."

"Well, my dear chameleon, you've come to the right place," Terrence replied, chuckling at Charlie's vibrant color-changing antics. "Tell me, what seems to be the problem?"

Charlie leaned closer, and in hushed tones, he whispered, "I'm worried about my taxes as I approach retirement. How can I mitigate them and still enjoy my golden years?"

Terrence stroked his chin thoughtfully and replied, "Ah, tax mitigation is a tricky dance indeed, my friend. However, fear not, for I have a fable for you, a story that will illustrate the importance of tax planning."

The animals gathered around in anticipation as Terrence launched into his fable.

Once upon a time, in a land not so far away, lived a group of hardworking ants who had spent their lives diligently saving for their golden years. They had built a vast network of underground tunnels to store their precious wealth, and they were proud of their accomplishments.

One day, as a harsh winter storm hit the land, the ants realized that the entrance to their tunnels had collapsed under the weight of the snow. Panic ensued! They had no way of accessing their savings to survive the winter.

But among the ants was a clever chameleon named Clarence. He was not only a master of disguise but also an expert in underground engineering. Clarence, realizing the gravity of the situation, stepped forward and offered a solution. He promised to repair the entrance to their tunnels and even build new secret entrances, ensuring their savings would never be inaccessible again.

The ants were thrilled! They quickly appointed Clarence as their chief architect and followed his instructions diligently. Soon, their once-inaccessible savings were now safely protected, thanks to Clarence's clever design.

As Terrence finished his fable, he smiled at Charlie and said, "You see, my dear chameleon friend, just like Clarence, tax mitigation strategies can ingeniously protect your hard-earned wealth during retirement."

Charlie's eyes sparkled with understanding, and he chuckled, "Ah, Terrence, you always find a way to bring wisdom and amusement together!"

Terrence winked and replied, "My dear friend, here's a practical example: imagine you have a sizable retirement portfolio, and you're planning to withdraw a significant amount to cover your expenses. Without proper tax planning, those withdrawals can be subject to heavy taxes, reducing your overall income."

Charlie nodded, realizing the importance of tax mitigation in retirement planning. He marveled at Terrence's ability to simplify complex ideas with his entertaining fables.

As the sun began to set, the animals bid Terrence farewell, their minds swirling with newfound knowledge and excitement about their financial futures. Terrence, the wise tax turtle, contentedly retreated, knowing he had once again illuminated the path toward prosperity for his friends.

And so, my friends, the tale of Terrence, the Tax Turtle, and the Clever Chameleon came to an end. But the lessons it imparted about tax mitigation in retirement planning continued to spread throughout the land of Financia, ensuring that animals far and wide could enjoy their golden years with financial ease and a sprinkling of laughter.

Remember, dear reader, the importance of tax mitigation in your retirement planning cannot be overstated. Trust in clever strategies, seek wise advisors, and may your golden years be filled with joy, abundance, and a touch of financial fun.

Chapter 18: The Tale of Accumulation and Distribution: A Laugh-Out-Loud Guide to Retirement Planning

Once upon a time, in the bustling city of Fiscopolis, two best friends, Wally the Wise and Benny the Bold, set out on a great adventure. They had reached the golden years of their lives and decided it was time to plan for the future. Wally, an old owl known for his wisdom, preferred the approach of accumulation, while Benny, a mischievous squirrel, believed in the power of distribution.

Their journey began at the grand Fiscopolis Bank, where the head banker, Mr. Pennypincher, greeted them with a toothy smile. "Welcome, welcome! How can I assist you fine gentlemen today?"

Wally cleared his throat in his best scholarly fashion. "We've come for guidance on retirement planning, dear sir. We seek the path that leads to financial security."

Mr. Pennypincher's eyes twinkled with excitement. "Ah, retirement planning! The mighty question of accumulation or distribution. Allow me to tell you a tale!" He gestured for them to gather around.

"Once upon a time, there was a diligent ant named Alfredo, who saved every tiny crumb he found. His friends mocked him for his saving habits, but Alfredo paid no mind. When winter arrived, with its icy breath and relentless hunger, Alfredo basked in comfort, while his friends struggled."

Wally nodded with approval, but Benny's eyes sparkled with intrigue, eager to share his perspective. "But wait, dear Mr. Pennypincher! Allow me to tell my side of the story!"

The banker chuckled. "Very well, Benny the Bold, do enlighten us."

Benny took center stage, dramatically puffing up his chest. "In the same forest as Alfredo, there was a carefree grasshopper named Gracie, who danced merrily all day. Gracie believed in sharing her good fortune, often throwing lavish feasts with her friends. When winter arrived, Gracie had nothing left but her charm."

Wally and Benny glared at each other, playfully arguing their cases like old pals. Mr. Pennypincher intervened, eager to guide them to a balanced perspective. "My dear friends, retirement planning isn't just about accumulation or distribution. It's about finding harmony between both."

Confused, Wally scratched his feathery head. "But how, Mr. Pennypincher?"

The banker leaned in closer, his voice a conspiratorial whisper. "Let me share the tale of Harold the Hedgehog."

Wally and Benny leaned forward, eager to hear this new fable.

"Harold was a diligent saver, just like Alfredo. But he also knew the value of enjoying his golden years, just like Gracie. Harold saved diligently, but also set aside a portion for enjoyment, treating himself to little pleasures and memorable experiences."

Wally gasped, his eyes wide with excitement. "You mean… finding a balance?"

Mr. Pennypincher nodded sagely. "Exactly! Retirement planning is not only about accumulating enough to secure your future but also cherishing the present. We must save wisely but also savor life's small joys along the way. Financial security is essential, but so is happiness."

With newfound clarity, Wally and Benny thanked Mr. Pennypincher for his guidance. They set off on their next adventure, armed with the knowledge to create a balanced retirement plan that would ensure a secure and enjoyable future.

And so, dear reader, remember the tale of Wally the Wise and Benny the Bold. When planning for your own golden years, seek the perfect blend of accumulation and distribution. Save wisely, but don't forget to enjoy life's delightful moments along the way. And may your retirement be filled with joy, laughter, and an abundance of financial fun.

Chapter 19: The Adventures of Penny and the Fee Band

Once upon a time in the land of Financia, there lived a wise old turtle named Pennywise. Pennywise had spent his entire life saving and planning for his retirement, building a sturdy nest egg to ensure a comfortable future. But little did he know, the cunning Fee Bandit was plotting to take a significant portion of his hard-earned coins.

Pennywise was familiar with the concept of retirement products, each promising to help him grow his wealth while he enjoyed the golden years of his life. With curiosity approaching its peak, he set off on a quest to explore these magical remnants.

His journey led him deep into the Forest of Financial Fineprint, where he encountered a mischievous hedgehog named Seymour. Seymour was the underling of the notorious Fee Bandit and was known for his ability to spin golden tales, hiding the nasty surprise of fees within.

Curiosity piqued, Pennywise approached Seymour cautiously. "Greetings, good hedgehog. I seek knowledge about the retirement products that grace our land. Tell me, what secrets do they hold?"

Seymour, with a twinkle in his eye, replied, "Oh, wise turtle, the retirement products are like enchanted seas, with vast treasures hidden within. They promise great wealth, but beware, for my master, the Fee Bandit, lurks in the shadows, ready to snatch a portion of your fortune!"

Pennywise gasped, his eyes growing wide. "A Fee Bandit? Pray tell, Seymour, how does he steal from unsuspecting savers like me?"

Seymour chuckled slyly. "Oh, fee structure is his weapon of choice! He disguises them cleverly as if they were tiny imps lurking in every document. They dance inconspicuously into your retirement funds, devouring your potential earnings."

Pennywise's heart raced with fear and concern. "How can I avoid falling into their clutches, Seymour?"

Seymour winked mischievously. "The tale, my dear turtle, is about the power of fee awareness and transparency. Just as a knight needs armor to protect from his foes, you must equip yourself with knowledge. Demand clarity and understand the fee structure of any retirement product you consider. Ask about annual fees, account maintenance fees, investment fees, and the like. Hold the providers accountable!"

Pennywise listened attentively, realizing the importance of this revelation. "Thank you, Seymour! Your wisdom will save me from the Fee Bandit's grasp. Now, shall we find a way to put an end to his mischief together?"

Seymour nodded, a newfound resolve taking hold. "Indeed, wise turtle. Let us rally the other animals of Financia, united against the injustice of hidden fees. Together, we will ensure transparency and protect the future of all savers."

Word spread quickly through the forest, and a mighty army formed—a coalition of animals determined to bring fee transparency to retirement products. The Fee Bandit trembled with fear as he watched his potential victims, now armed with knowledge, stand tall and united.

And so it came to pass that, with the help of Pennywise, Seymour, and their trusty army, the Fee Bandit was banished from Financia forever. Retirement products became transparent, and savers all across the land rejoiced at their newfound ability to make well-informed decisions.

As Pennywise watched the sun set on Financia, he marveled at the power of fee transparency. His journey had taught him that understanding and managing fees was not just a way to protect his nest egg, but a vital step in securing a stable financial future.

And so, dear reader, let this fable be a cautionary tale—a reminder that in the realm of retirement planning, fee transparency is the armor that shields you from the clutches of the Fee Bandit. Arm yourself with knowledge, demand transparency, and may your financial future always be fortified.

Chapter 20: The Unraveling Yarn: A Hilarious Tale of Social Security's Future

Once upon a time, in a land not too far away, there existed a cozy town named Fiscally Fairytale. It was a place where the people liked to think they were living in perfect harmony with money, blissfully unaware of the comedic storm that was brewing.

In the heart of Fiscally Fairytale, there stood a grand, clock tower-like building known as the Social Security Administration, where the charming protagonist, Mr. Pennyworth, worked diligently to keep the spiraling yarn of Social Security from completely unraveling. Mr. Pennyworth was a quirky man with a gray mustache that always quivered when he got nervous.

One fine morning, as Mr. Pennyworth settled into his cubicle, he heard a commotion in the hallway. Bursting through the door with a flurry of papers was the impulsive Mayor Quibbleton, a man known for his grandiose ideas but complete lack of understanding about finances.

"Mr. Pennyworth, I demand that you fix Social Security right away!" Mayor Quibbleton declared, panting heavily.

Mr. Pennyworth was taken aback. "But, Your Honor, fixing Social Security is like knitting a giant tapestry! It takes time, patience, and wise decision-making."

"Well, we can't wait for wisdom!" the mayor huffed as he began pacing. "I propose we throw a huge party and invite all the townspeople to dance away our financial troubles!"

Amused, Mr. Pennyworth raised an eyebrow. "But, Your Honor, dancing isn't a solution."

Ignoring Mr. Pennyworth's wise words, the mayor sprung into action, organizing a dance party complete with a live band, a jester, and even a clumsy tightrope walker. The people of Fiscally Fairytale danced and laughed, temporarily forgetting their financial worries.

However, as the sun set on the party, reality crept back in. The town coffers were empty, leaving Mayor Quibbleton scratching his head and Mr. Pennyworth sighing in exasperation.

Just as all hope seemed lost, a peculiar figure strode into the Social Security Administration building. It was Jestine, the vibrant yet scatterbrained accountant who had a remarkable talent for making sense out of numbers.

"You're in luck!" Jestine exclaimed, her rainbow-colored dress shimmering in the sunlight. "I've figured out a plan to fix Social Security!"

Mr. Pennyworth and the mayor exchanged skeptical glances, but they were desperate enough to listen to Jestine's amusing proposal. She explained that they could fund Social Security by pitting unicorns against dragons in a thrilling race around Fiscally Fairytale. The townspeople would gather to watch and bet, with the proceeds going toward securing Social Security's future.

"Unicorns and dragons? Betting on a race?" Mr. Pennyworth chuckled. "This is utter nonsense!"

But Mayor Quibbleton, ever the optimist, embraced the idea. "Brilliant! Why, the townspeople will have a hoot, and our finances will be saved!"

With a whirlwind of colors and much ado, Jestine set to work organizing the mythical creature race. Posters of fire-breathing dragons and graceful unicorns adorned every inch of Fiscally Fairytale.

As the race day arrived, the townspeople flooded the streets, cheering wildly for their chosen creature. Unicorns leaped majestically, their horns glistening, while dragons soared through the air, sparks flying from their nostrils. The chaos and excitement were palpable.

At the finish line, Mayor Quibbleton presented the prize money to the proud unicorn owners, who were delighted to contribute a portion to Social Security. As the crowd erupted with applause, Mr. Pennyworth couldn't help but smile. Maybe Jestine's absurd idea hadn't been so foolish after all.

So, the unraveling yarn of Social Security was temporarily mended, and the town of Fiscally Fairytale learned a valuable lesson. Fixing Social Security required more than dancing or mythical creature races; it needed careful planning, sensible decisions, and a touch of creativity.

And as Mr. Pennyworth basked in the bittersweet triumph, he couldn't help but hope that the quirky people of Fiscally Fairytale would remember this tale and apply its lessons to their own financial lives.

Thus, the future of Social Security remained uncertain, but at least the people understood that a dash of humor, a pinch of absurdity, and a lot of common sense could help them face the challenges ahead. And so, the town of Fiscally Fairytale continued to dance its way through life, one whimsical step at a time.

Chapter 21: The Aristocratic Ant and the Mischievous Mouse – A Tale of Average Returns versus Real Returns

Once upon a time, in a vibrant meadow full of blooming flowers and towering trees, lived an industrious ant named Alfred. Alfred prided himself on his hard work, always diligently collecting bits of grain for the winter ahead. He was known throughout the meadow for his impeccable sense of planning and his unwavering commitment to financial stability.

On the flip side, there was a mischievous little mouse named Monty, whose idea of a good time involved feasting on the fruits of others' labor. He rejected the concept of saving for a rainy day, believing life should be an endless party.

One sunny day, as Alfred was busily engaged in his routine work of securing a heap of grains for the winter, Monty approached him, a look of sheer delight etched across his whiskered face.

"Dear Alfred, my friend, why do you waste your days working so hard?" Monty exclaimed between bites of a stolen apple. "The world is a grand playground full of berries and seeds waiting to be enjoyed! Why bother hoarding grain? Come and join me on my quest for adventure!"

Alfred paused for a moment, assessing Monty's words. Although tempted by the carefree nature of his friend's lifestyle, he knew better than to succumb to momentary gratification. His sharp, analytical mind propelled him to dig deeper into Monty's seductive proposal.

"Ah, Monty, isn't it true that you only consider the immediate pleasures of the present? What about the harsh winter that inevitably follows? While you frolic and enjoy the ephemeral joys, I endeavor to secure a stable future for myself," Alfred replied with a hint of concern in his voice.

Monty chuckled, his whiskers twitching mischievously. "But dear Alfred, do you not see that I am living life to its fullest? A life spent only preparing for the inevitable is not a life worth living! Oh, how I pity your innumerable grains and your meticulous plans."

The mouse's playful taunts weighed heavily on Alfred's mind. Doubt began to creep into his resolute nature. Perhaps Monty was right; perhaps all his laborious efforts were in vain. Intrigued by Monty's audacious claims, Alfred decided to ponder the idea further.

So, the two embarked on a journey to the nearby trading post where they met Wilbur, a wise old owl who doubled as a market enthusiast and a financial advisor.

Alfred and Monty presented their dilemmas to Wilbur, who listened attentively. He stroked his feathery chin, deep in thought. Finally, he spoke:

"Ah! My dear friends, it seems we have stumbled upon a classic conundrum in the world of finance – average returns versus real returns!"

Seeing the confusion on their faces, Wilbur began explaining with a twinkle in his eyes, knowing that he had found the perfect audience for his favorite fable.

"Imagine," Wilbur began, "that there are two enchanted trees in this meadow, each producing luscious fruits. The first tree, which we shall call the 'Average Tree,' produces precisely five ripe, juicy fruits every year without fail. The second tree, the 'Real Tree,' has some wild swings in its production. Some years it yields no fruit, other years it may produce a bountiful twelve fruits."

Alfred and Monty listened, captivated by the analogy.

"You see, Alfred," Wilbur continued, "the Average Tree represents average returns. It consistently offers five fruits every year, much like an average return on an investment. On the other hand, the Real Tree shows the volatility of real returns. It may produce a significant amount of fruits, but in some years, it might disappoint with little or no yield."

Suddenly, Monty's eyes widened as he began to understand the implications of his carefree lifestyle. He realized that, much like the Real Tree, he could feast like royalty during good years, but when lean times came, he would suffer the consequences of his recklessness.

Alfred, reassured by this newfound knowledge, smiled. He finally saw the true value in his hard work and his diligent planning. Understanding the difference between average returns and real returns presented him with a powerful tool to navigate his financial future wisely.

As the trio parted ways, Alfred returned to his grain collection with renewed zeal. Monty, now enlightened, decided to make small lifestyle changes, ensuring he could revel in the present without jeopardizing his future.

So, dear readers, let this tale be a reminder of the importance of understanding average returns versus real returns. It is a lesson that, even in the wondrous world of finance, can be discovered through the magic of friendship, clever trinkets, and the wisdom of a wise old owl.

Chapter 22: The Misadventures of APR and EIC

Once upon a time, in the land of Financia, two friends, APR and EIC, lived side by side. APR, a mischievous monkey, loved to swing from tree to tree, while EIC, a witty and wise owl, perched on a branch nearby, always with a book in hand.

One sunny day, APR swung down excitedly, holding a shiny balloon he had found in the village square. He approached EIC with a big grin, saying, "Hey, EIC! Look what I found! It's a magical balloon that makes money!"

EIC raised an eyebrow in disbelief, but nevertheless, he leaned in to examine the balloon. "APR, my friend," EIC cautioned, "Before we get carried away, let me explain how this 'magic' works. You know, with our roles as financial wizards, we cannot afford any misunderstandings."

APR scratched his head, taking a moment to grasp EIC's words. "Okay, wise owl, enlighten me."

EIC cleared his throat and began, "Well, my dear friend, APR stands for Annual Percentage Rate. It's like your monkey charm and attracts people with its enticing numbers. You see, it's used to represent the interest rate on a loan annually, along with any additional charges."

APR's eyes widened, realizing that this shiny balloon of his might have more to it than he initially thought. "Okay, okay, but what about EIC then?"

"EIC, my friend, is short for Effective Interest Cost," explained EIC, adjusting his spectacles. "It represents the actual cost of borrowing over the entire loan term, factoring in the compounding of interest, fees, and other charges associated with the loan."

APR scratched his furry chin in puzzlement. "So, you're telling me that APR is like the surface-level attraction, and EIC, well, it's like the whole package, huh?"

EIC chuckled, nodding in agreement. "Exactly, APR may seem appealing on the surface, but EIC shows the true cost over time. It's crucial to understand both to make an informed financial decision."

Intrigued by this newfound knowledge, APR returned to the village square, holding his shiny balloon high in the sky. Word spread quickly about this magical balloon that made money, and people from all around Financia flocked to see it.

Among the crowd was a sheep named Baa-rney, known for his impulsive nature. Seeing APR's balloon, his eyes sparkled with greed. "APR! APR! I must have that balloon! How much should I pay for it?"

APR grinned mischievously, pointing to a small price tag tied to the balloon's string. "Just 5 exuberant giggles, my friend!"

Baa-rney's eyes widened, and he handed over the giggles without hesitation, eager to possess the magic balloon.

Little did Baa-rney know, APR had overlooked the fine print. The APR balloon had a high interest rate that compounded daily, and it would eventually become a financial nightmare for poor Baa-rney.

As months passed, the APR balloon proved to be a burden. The compounding interest and hidden charges made Baa-rney's wallet suffer, and he struggled to make the monthly payments. He soon realized that without understanding the EIC, he had been trapped in a cycle of debt.

APR, feeling guilty about his scheme, approached EIC for advice. "My friend, EIC, I've made a mess of things! How can we help poor Baa-rney out of this predicament?"

EIC pondered for a moment, then smiled. "We need to educate our friend Baa-rney about the significance of EIC. With this knowledge, he can compare different loan options and make a more informed choice."

Together, APR and EIC ventured back to the village square, armed with pamphlets, banners, and a giant stage. They organized a lively town hall meeting, explaining the difference between APR and EIC in an engaging and hilarious way.

As the villagers listened, laughter filled the air, making the information all the more memorable. From then on, APR and EIC became beloved comedy duo of Financia, using their wit and charm to enlighten and save the village from financial mishaps.

And so, dear reader, as APR and EIC continued their adventures, they reminded everyone in Financia of the importance of understanding the distinction between APR and EIC—a lesson that echoed throughout the land for generations to come.

Chapter 23 - Debt elimination by Debt Snowballing

Once upon a time, in the charming town of Debtopia, there lived two best friends named Fred and George. These two were always getting into wild adventures, but one day they found themselves in a situation they couldn't escape – debt!

Debtopia was known for its tempting bakeries, and Fred, being a self-proclaimed pastry connoisseur, could never resist indulging in a cream-filled donut. George, on the other hand, had a weakness for the latest gadgets and would often be seen waving a shiny new phone around. Their desires got the better of them, and both friends found themselves drowning in credit card debt.

One sunny morning, Fred and George decided it was high time to take control of their finances. They stumbled upon a secret book called "The Debt Whisperer," rumored to have the power to turn debt into dust. Excited, they flipped to a chapter about a concept called the "debt snowball." It sounded intriguing, but first, they needed to find someone who could decipher the cryptic teachings within its pages.

Enter Mr. Moneybags, the renowned financial advisor of Debtopia. He had an aura of wisdom, despite his peculiar habit of wearing a top hat with a dollar sign on it. With a twinkle in his eye and a mischievous smile, Mr. Moneybags agreed to help Fred and George climb out of their debt mountain.

"So, my dear friends, the debt snowball is a simple yet effective technique," began Mr. Moneybags. "You start by listing all your debts from smallest to largest, regardless of interest rates."

"Smallest?" George looked puzzled. "But won't the higher-interest ones cost us more in the long run?"

Fred scratched his head and nodded in agreement, "Yeah, it sounds counterintuitive."

Mr. Moneybags chuckled, "Ah, but it's all about momentum and motivation! When you pay off the smallest debt first, you gain a sense of accomplishment, giving you the confidence to tackle the bigger ones. It's a psychological trick that keeps you motivated."

Fred's eyes widened, and George nodded in understanding. "That's clever! But how do we incorporate whole life insurance into this magical debt-elimination journey?" asked Fred, a hint of skepticism in his voice.

Taking a dramatic pause, Mr. Moneybags dramatically spun his top hat on his finger. "Whole life insurance, my inquisitive friends, is our secret weapon. It accumulates cash value over time, which can be used to pay off debts or support your loved ones if anything happens to you."

"But how does it work?" George asked, intrigued.

"Well," said Mr. Moneybags, grinning, "as you make premium payments for your whole life insurance, the cash value grows. You can take out loans against this value and use it to pay off your debts. Plus, it provides a safety net in case of emergencies, ensuring the debt monster won't rear its ugly head again."

Fred and George exchanged glances, their eyes gleaming with

newfound determination. "We're sold! Let's eliminate this debt!"

And so, armed with the debt snowball method and whole life insurance, Fred and George embarked on their adventure. They started by paying off a school loan that was as ancient as the town itself. The satisfaction of shredding the final loan statement was indescribable! They celebrated with a batch of celebratory debt-free donuts, clearly made from guilt-free ingredients.

As they continued to pay off their debts one by one, Fred and George found themselves liberated from the financial stresses that plagued their lives. Along the way, they encountered amusing situations like accidentally saving their coupons only to use them years after their expiration dates or discovering a hidden stash of forgotten pennies under their couch cushions.

Their journey wasn't without its challenges, but their determination and the ongoing advice from Mr. Moneybags kept them on track. Through witty dialogues and comedic mishaps, the chapter showcased the debt snowball method and whole life insurance as a dynamic duo that obliterated debt with a hint of laughter.

At the end of this captivating chapter, readers were left inspired and entertained, itching to implement the debt snowball method and explore the power of whole life insurance. As Fred and George triumphantly waved their debt-free flags, readers were nudged to take their steps toward financial freedom and bid adieu to debt once and for all.

Chapter 24: The Great Debt Debate

Once upon a time, in the quaint town of Pennyville, there lived two charismatic characters who were known far and wide for their love of debates. They were none other than Good Debt and Bad Debt, and boy, did they have some opinions about their respective roles in people's lives.

Good Debt, a dapper fellow with a top hat and a pristine suit, considered himself the hero of the financial world. He believed in using borrowed money to invest in oneself, like acquiring an education or starting a business. Bad Debt, on the other hand, was a sly and mischievous chap who wore a flashy outfit and carried a credit card that never left his grasp. He viewed himself as the life of the party, promoting impulsive spending and frivolous acquisitions.

One sunny afternoon, the town gathered in the local square for the highly anticipated Great Debt Debate. Good Debt and Bad Debt took center stage, ready to woo the audience with their wit and arguments.

"I bring you financial freedom and prosperity," Good Debt proclaimed confidently. "Through me, you can pursue higher education and open doors to better job opportunities."

Bad Debt chuckled and sidled up to the podium. "Ah, my dear friends, it is I who brings you instant gratification and a lifestyle of luxury. Why save for years to buy that shiny new gadget when you can swipe your card and have it in an instant?"

The crowd murmured, undecided about who had the more

enticing proposition. Sensing the tension, the town's mayor stepped forward and declared, "Let's settle this with a series of challenges! Show us the consequences of your choices, and we shall decide who carries more weight."

Game on.

In the first challenge, the mayor instructed both characters to help a young couple pursue their dream of owning a home. Good Debt confidently guided the couple to take out a mortgage with manageable interest rates, ensuring they could afford monthly payments while making a sound investment for their future. The couple marveled at their new home, grateful to Good Debt for imparting his wisdom.

Bad Debt, though, had an entirely different plan. He persuaded the couple to splurge on an extravagant mansion beyond their means, borrowing way more than they could pay back. The couple soon found themselves drowning in debt, unable to keep up with the extravagant lifestyle they could ill afford. Their dream house became a nightmare, thanks to Bad Debt's tricks.

Round one undeniably swayed the audience in favor of Good Debt, but Bad Debt remained undeterred and confident as ever. He was determined to win them over.

For the next challenge, the mayor summoned two recent graduates, eager to start their careers. Good Debt encouraged them to take out a reasonable student loan, investing in their skills to obtain higher-paying jobs in the future. The graduates embraced Good Debt's advice and embarked on their promising career paths.

Bad Debt, of course, had other plans. He convinced the same graduates to finance their extravagant lifestyles with excessive credit card debt, carelessly ignoring the consequences of high interest rates. Within months, they found themselves buried under a mountain of debt, forced to work multiple jobs just to stay afloat.

The crowd watched and laughed as Bad Debt frantically tried to avoid the debt collectors chasing him around the square. It was clear that his irresistible charm had failed him this time.

In a surprising twist, the mayor announced a final challenge: a real-life financial crisis. He wanted to see if Good Debt and Bad Debt could weather the storm and truly prove their worth in the toughest of times.

Good Debt, ever the visionary, encouraged people to prioritize their needs, save for emergencies, and invest wisely while weathering the storm. People who heeded his advice kept their heads above water, retaining their financial stability.

Bad Debt, on the other hand, had a difficult time convincing anyone to follow him. His incessant desire for instant gratification had left him with no credibility. People sought refuge in their savings and vowed to never again succumb to his tricks.

The Great Debt Debate had come to an end, and it was evident that Good Debt had emerged as the victor. The townsfolk marveled at their newfound knowledge of financial responsibility, having been entertained while learning valuable lessons along the way.

As the curtain fell on this lively fable, the people of Pennyville couldn't help but be grateful for the laughter, entertainment, and wit that had enlightened them on the importance of distinguishing between good and bad debt. They resolved to apply these lessons in their own lives, ensuring a financially secure future.

And so, dear readers, remember to laugh, learn, and think twice before becoming entangled in the manipulative grip of Bad Debt. After all, the path to financial freedom is paved with the wise choices of Good Debt.

Chapter 25: The Wily Fox and the Well-Preserved Business

Once upon a time, in the bustling town of Curtopia, there lived a clever fox named Oscar. Oscar was well-known for his cunning ways and sharp wit, traits that helped him thrive in the cut-throat world of business. However, his latest venture had hit a snag, and he found himself face-to-face with the great challenge of business preservation.

You see, Oscar had opened a bakery called "The Sly Patisserie," known far and wide for itslectable pastries and mouthwatering treats. But lately, a rival bakery had emerged, threatening to steal away customers and drive The Sly Patisserie to ruin.

One sunny morning, as Oscar pondered his predicament, a wise old owl named Ophelia flew in through the bakery's open window. Spotting Oscar's furrowed brow, she perched on a flour-dusted counter and asked, "Why the long face, Oscar? You look more sourdough than sourdough bread."

With a sigh, Oscar replied, "Dear Ophelia, my business is in peril. This rival bakery threatens to crumble my empire of pastries and take away my loyal customers. I am at a loss."

Ophelia blinked her big, round eyes, pondering his words for a moment. Then, a gleam of wisdom flickered within her gaze. "Ah, Oscar! You must remember that preservation is key in business. Think of a jar of pickles, my friend. The secret to their longevity lies in their preservation. You should do the same!"

Oscar's face lit up like an oven, and he thanked Ophelia for her sage advice. With newfound determination, he set off to devise a plan to preserve his business's success.

First, Oscar decided to spice up his menu. He introduced a tantalizing array of new pastries, each more scrumptious than the last. There were creamy custard rolls, buttery croissants filled with exotic fruits, and even a cinnamon twist named "The Circling Serpent." These new creations set The Sly Patisserie apart from its competition, drawing customers in like bees to a honey pot.

Next, Oscar took to the streets, personally handing out samples. He dubbed himself "The Sneaky Salesfox" and roamed the town wearing a cape made from discarded pastry bags. With a twinkle in his eye and a mischievous grin, he offered passerby tiny pastries on miniature silver platters, ensuring they tasted the delectable delights of The Sly Patisserie.

But the rival bakery wasn't one to be outfoxed easily. They retaliated by lowering their prices. Oscar knew he had to keep his customers loyal, so he devised yet another clever plan. He introduced a loyalty program called "The Cunning Club." For every tenth purchase, customers received a ticket to attend an exclusive bakers' carnival, where sugar-sprinkled donkeys would take them for rides and bakers juggled with delicious pastries amid cheers and laughter. This remarkable initiative had customers two-stepping down the streets to The Sly Patisserie, their bellies rumbling for pastries.

Weeks passed, and the rival bakery's efforts wilted like day-old bread. Oscar's well-preserved business was thriving, and the rival's bakers were left scratching their heads—though they did manage to invent a new line of itchy bread, but that's a tale for another day.

As the town's residents enjoyed pastries from The Sly Patisserie, they marveled at Oscar's ingenuity. No one could handle a doughy dilemma quite like that sly fox. And so, the townspeople learned the importance of preserving a business through wit and innovation.

The moral of the story? In the world of business, one must be as sly as a fox. A well-crafted plan to preserve your business will keep the dough rolling, even when faced with rival bakeries or stiff competition. After all, as Oscar so cleverly realized, if you can't beat 'em, outfox 'em!

And so, dear reader, the tale of Oscar and his well-preserved business reminds us to use our wits and ingenuity to keep our businesses thriving. The world may be filled with challenges and pitfalls, but with a dash of cunning and a pinch of innovation, we can preserve the businesses we hold dear, ensuring a sweeter future for all.

Chapter 26: The Greedy Hare and the Sly Tortoise

Once upon a time, in the lively land of Financialopolis, there lived a greedy hare named Harold and a sly tortoise named Theodore. Harold was always on the lookout for a quick way to become rich without lifting a paw. Theodore, the clever tortoise, saw this as an opportunity to teach Harold a valuable lesson about the dangers of get-rich-quick schemes.

One sunny day, as Harold was hopping through the marketplace, he stumbled upon a crowd gathered around a booth. Curiosity piqued, he hopped on over to see what all the fuss was about. There, behind the booth, stood the charismatic fox, Fredrick, who claimed to have discovered a magical secret to becoming rich overnight.

"Step right up, my friends!" Fredrick proclaimed with a sneaky grin. "With just a small investment, I will share my secret with you and guarantee untold riches!"

Harold's ears perked up, and his whiskers wiggled with excitement. He whispered to himself, "This is it! My ticket to everlasting wealth!" Without a second thought, he handed over his hard-earned carrots to Fredrick and eagerly awaited his magical secret.

Fredrick handed Harold a box filled with sparkling gemstones. "These magical gemstones possess the power to multiply your wealth tenfold. All you need to do is bury them under a full moon, and riches will come flooding your way," Fredrick whispered mischievously.

Overjoyed, Harold followed Fredrick's instructions meticulously. He dug a deep hole and buried the gemstones under the shimmering light of the full moon. With dreams of a lavish carrot-filled life dancing in his head, Harold eagerly awaited his wealth to multiply before his eyes.

Days turned into weeks, and weeks turned into months, but Harold's fortune seemed to be nowhere in sight. Theodore, watching from the sidelines, couldn't help but chuckle at Harold's gullibility.

"You didn't honestly believe that magical gemstones would multiply your wealth, did you?" Theodore said with a knowing smile.

Harold's ears drooped, and his heart sank. "Was it all a trick? Have I been deceived?" Harold lamented.

Theodore nodded sympathetically. "Indeed, my friend, the road to riches is not paved with easy shortcuts. Trust me when I say that true wealth comes from hard work, integrity, and making smart financial decisions."

Harold realized his foolishness and thanked Theodore for his wise words. From that day forward, Harold vowed to work diligently and make thoughtful financial choices that would lead to real and lasting prosperity.

And so, the moral of this fable is clear: Beware the allure of get-rich-quick schemes, for they are often empty promises that lead to disappointment and despair. True wealth and success are achieved through honest work and wise investments, not deceitful shortcuts.

As the hare and the tortoise continued their journey through Financialopolis, they shared their fable with others, reminding all who would listen to separate myth from truth and to never fall victim to the enticing traps of quick wealth through deceptive means.

And so, dear reader, remember this fable's tale and spread the word: Be patient, work hard, and invest wisely, and true financial success will be yours!

Chapter 27: Investment Follies: Tales of Financial Misadventures and Laughable Lessons

Once upon a time, in a bustling village called Pennyworth, there lived a group of animals with nothing but ambition and dollar signs in their heads. These lively creatures, who prided themselves on their sharp animal instincts, decided to enter the whimsical world of investments. Little did they know, a wild rollercoaster ride awaited them, filled with hilarious misadventures and laughable lessons.

Enter Barmy Billy the Bull, a lively character with an unwavering obsession for "get-rich-quick" schemes, and Freddy the Fox, who fancied himself as the wisest animal in the village. Together, they embarked on a quest to outsmart the market and make a fortune that would put King Midas to shame.

Their first stop was a small, dusty investment boutique run by a wise old tortoise named Oliver. Oliver welcomed the duo with a somber smile, as he had met many ambitious animals like them before.

"Welcome, young ones," Oliver mumbled. "Tell me, what brings you to my humble abode?"

Billy, grinning ear to ear, exclaimed, "We want to invest and make oodles of money! We heard you're the wisest animal in all of Pennyworth."

Oliver chuckled, shaking his shell gently. "Beware, my friends, investing is a delicate dance. Many have tried to conquer the market and have fallen flat on their hooves or paws."

"No worries, old chap. We got it all figured out," Freddy the Fox chimed in, smirking. "We've got a secret formula for success!"

Billy leaned over, whispering into Oliver's ear. "Come closer, old tortoise, we've discovered the secret indicator of a reliable investment: the Magic Feather Index!"

Oliver raised an eyebrow, bemused. "Magic Feather Index? Pray tell, what is this wondrous element?"

"It's simple," Billy proclaimed, waggling his horns. "Whenever we see a feather falling from the sky, we invest in the market. It's never failed us!"

Oliver's laughter filled the air, causing the birds perched on branches nearby to flutter away. "My dear friends, investments require careful consideration, not whimsical signs from the heavens. Come, let me tell you the tale of the Hasty Hedgehog."

Once upon another time, in a neighboring village, the Hasty Hedgehog was renowned for his hasty decisions. Convinced he possessed boundless animal instinct, he invested his fortune in the booming acorn industry.

But alas, the acorn bubble burst, leaving the Hasty Hedgehog scrambling to recoup his losses. The moral of this tale, my curious companions, is to let rationality guide your investments, not the whims of feathers or bubbles.

Billy and Freddy exchanged amused glances, realizing the folly of their Magic Feather Index. Oliver had successfully shaken their misplaced confidence.

Humbled but determined, the duo left the tortoise's humble abode, deciding they needed a dose of sanity. They stumbled upon a meeting held by the venerable owl, Professor Wisebeak, renowned for his sage insights into financial markets.

As Professor Wisebeak's monotone voice droned on, Billy's eyes began to glaze over. Freddy, on the other hand, nudged Billy awake. "Listen up, Billy," he whispered. "I might have just discovered the secret to success."

With glints of excitement in his eyes Billy leaned closer. "What is it, Freddy?"

"A surefire investment, my friend," Freddy whispered conspiratorially. "The key to success is investing in the companies that produce the most donuts. Everyone loves donuts!"

Billy burst into laughter, snorting wildly. "That's it? Donuts? You've lost your mind, Freddy!"

As the laughter subsided, they heard the sage owl's final words: "Remember, my dear animals, clever investments are grounded in thorough research and understanding, not in the flakiest of pastries."

Billy and Freddy exchanged sheepish glances, realizing that they had indeed lost their minds.

With lessons learned and egos deflated, Billy and Freddy returned to the village of Pennyworth, embracing a new mantra:

"Invest responsibly, learn from the wise, and never chase feathered whims or frosted dreams."

And so, dear readers, the lesson from this fable is etched in the annals of Pennyworth village. Embrace the wisdom that investing requires careful consideration, knowledge, and a healthy sense of humor. May your investments be fruitful, and may laughter guide you through every financial adventure.

Chapter 28: The Tale of the Wise Ostrich and the Three Annuities

Once upon a time, in the bustling town of Financeville, there lived a wise and undeniably fabulous ostrich named Olivia. Olivia had a reputation for being the go-to advisor for all things financially fantastic. People would flock from far and wide to seek her wisdom and guidance.

One sunny day, a group of curious critters gathered around Olivia, eager to learn about the mysterious world of annuities. Olivia, always up for a challenge, decided to enlighten her audience using her favorite teaching technique – fables!

"Picture this," Olivia began, as the critters leaned in closer. "In the heart of Financeville, there was a great marketplace where three annuities resided – Fixed, Fixed Index, and Variable. Let's meet the lovely annuities and see how they each fared."

First, she introduced the Fixed Annuity named Fred. Fred was a diligent ant with an extraordinary sense of organization. He liked to keep things simple and predictable for everyone around him. "Fred," Olivia chuckled, "was the consistent rhythm of the marketplace. He knew exactly how much interest he would yield, and his payments never wavered. Just like a trustworthy ticking clock, Fred provided a steady stream of income to those in need."

Next, Olivia introduced the Fixed Index Annuity called Fiona. Fiona was a sprightly squirrel with a knack for trying new things. She loved the thrill of the chase, the excitement of adventure. Fiona, unlike her fixed sibling Fred, wasn't content with just being predictable. "Fiona," Olivia exclaimed, "was like a tiny acrobat, always looking for ways to take advantage of market growth, without exposing herself to too much risk. Her payments could increase based on the performance of a market index, like a trapeze artist soaring to new heights!"

Finally, Olivia introduced the Variable Annuity named Victor – a cheeky chameleon who was never one to shy away from risk. Victor thrived on the unknown, always seeking opportunities that might make the timid creatures tremble. "Victor," Olivia declared, with a twinkle in her eye, "offered the potential for greater returns, but at a price. His payments fluctuated wildly depending on market performance, and he required a brave soul to ride the roller coaster of ever-changing fortunes."

The critters were captivated by Olivia's storytelling abilities, their little eyes sparkling with enthusiasm.

"Isn't it marvelous," Olivia continued, "how annuities cater to everyone's unique needs? Whether you value stability, controlled adventure, or living life on the edge, there's an annuity for you!"

"But how do these annuities truly differ?" timidly asked a shrew named Sally.

Olivia smiled knowingly. She led the critters over to an enormous pie, filled with equally enormous slices. "Imagine," she began, "that this delicious pie represents your retirement savings. Now, Fred the Fixed Annuity would give you a fabulous slice, but always the same size, every month. Fiona the Fixed Index Annuity, on the other hand, would offer you a small slice to start but could grow bigger with time. Meanwhile, Victor the Variable Annuity would give you a slice that could fluctuate greatly, just like a wild roller-coaster ride."

The critters nodded, their stomachs rumbling with both under-standing and hunger.

Olivia concluded, "In the end, the decision to choose an annu-ity depends on your appetite for risk and desire for potential growth. Do you prefer a steady slice, a controlled adventure, or a heart-pounding roller-coaster ride?"

Just as the critters pondered Olivia's words, the marketplace burst into laughter. Fred had organized a parade with animals holding gigantic ticking clocks, Fiona had set up a carnival filled with acrobatic squirrels, and Victor was conducting a live rock concert with chameleons dressed in ever-changing dazzling outfits.

And so, dear readers, remember that annuities, like the wise Os-trich's tale, can both educate and entertain. Choose wisely, and may your financial future be filled with joyous surprises, regard-less of the annuity path you choose!

Chapter 29: The Tale of Two Investments

Once upon a time, in the bustling kingdom of Financiere, there lived two investments named Stocks and Bonds. Stocks was a flamboyant character, always chasing dreams of grandeur and indulging in risky adventures. Bonds, on the other hand, was prudent and cautious, preferring a reliable and steady life.

Stocks, with his unruly hair and energetic demeanor, was charismatic and captivating. He roamed the kingdom, introducing himself to everyone he met, charming them with promises of great fortune. "Invest in me," he said, "and you shall reap the rewards of a booming market!"

Bonds, on the contrary, was reserved and polished, with a bowtie that was the talk of the town. He approached potential investors with a calm demeanor, gently reassuring them, "Place your trust in me, and I shall protect your wealth like a knight in shining armor."

Amidst the kingdom's cafes, Stocks and Bonds would often meet to discuss their differences. Stocks would boast about the exhilarating highs and devastating lows of his adventurous life. "Ah, my friend," he'd say, "I can make you rich overnight! But you must also be prepared to stomach the weight of uncertainty."

Bonds, ever the cautious creature, nodded thoughtfully. "Indeed, my dear Stocks, you offer great excitement, but what about stability? While I may not give you immediate riches, I can guarantee regular income and a more secure future."

As their conversations continued, the two investments gathered a cohort of loyal followers. Stocks had a band of risk-loving knights, ready to face any challenge for the promise of sky-high returns. Bonds, pensive and reliable, attracted a group of loyal guards, appreciative of the comfort and safety he offered.

One sunny day, at the Great Financial Academy, Stocks and Bonds were invited to showcase their talents. The audience, a mix of young adventurers and cautious souls, eagerly awaited their performances.

Stocks leaped onto the stage with grandeur, arms flailing and voice booming. He flashed colorful charts, pointing to the possibilities of untold wealth. "Buy low, sell high! The world is yours, my friends!" he exclaimed. The crowd cheered and their eyes sparkled with dreams.

Then, it was Bonds' turn. Stepping onto the stage with his polished shoes, Bonds projected an air of reliability. He presented a simple graph, a slow progression upwards. "With me, dear investors, you will have the peace of mind that comes from steady income and capital preservation," he declared. The audience nodded, impressed with the promise of stability.

As the tale unfolded, the audience soon realized the contrasting nature of Stocks and Bonds. Stocks certainly had the potential for remarkable growth and enticing returns, but he was prone to volatility and unpredictable swings. Bonds, on the other hand, might not provide jaw-dropping gains, but he acted as a reliable buffer, cushioning the blows of economic uncertainties.

In the end, every investor had a choice to make, a balance to find between Stocks' promise of excitement and the security offered by Bonds. Some chose to dance with Stocks, embracing the thrill of his adventures. Others clung to Bonds, seeking solace in the certainty he provided.

The moral of this whimsical tale is to understand that diversification and balance are key in any financial strategy. While Stocks may offer great potential, one must not neglect the protective shield of Bonds. By blending the two, investors can build a robust portfolio that can weather the stormy seas of the market while still seeking the rewards of fruitful investments.

And so, dear readers, remember this: Do not let yourself be swayed solely by dreams of grandeur or crushed under the weight of caution. Seek the perfect harmony between the adventurous spirit of Stocks and the reliable nature of Bonds, and you shall navigate the kingdom of Financiere with wisdom and prosperity.

Chapter 30: The Tale of the Dancing Dollars: Unraveling the Perils of Sequence of Returns Risks

Once upon a time in the quaint town of Moneyville, lived a lively cast of characters who had one thing in common—they were all on a quest to secure their financial futures. In this whimsical chapter of "Financial Fun: Separating Myth from Truth in Hilarious Fables," we unveil the story of a wild adventure through the unexpected twists and turns of financial planning, led by the flamboyant Professor Pennyworth.

Our story begins a sunny day in the heart of Moneyville, where Professor Pennyworth struts through the town square, clinking his cane and twirling his handlebar mustache. With his colorful attire and boisterous personality, Pennyworth certainly knows how to draw a crowd.

"I have the answer to all your financial worries!" he exclaims, capturing the eager attention of the gathered townsfolk. "But beware, for lurking in the shadows is a sneaky foe known as the Sequence of Returns Risk."

A murmur of curiosity sweeps through the crowd. Their eyes widen, hungry for knowledge. But how can such a stuffy topic be transformed into an engaging tale? Fear not, for Pennyworth has a way with words.

As the story unfolds, we meet our protagonist, Jack the Jester. Jack has always dreamt of having a grand fortune, so he seeks out Pennyworth's wisdom. Eager to guide Jack from the path of financial ruin, Pennyworth conjures a magical spreadsheet that visualizes the sequence of returns over multiple years.

At the flick of a wand (or merely the stroke of a finger on a touchpad), the spreadsheet comes alive with dancing dollar signs, spinning in jubilant circles. The townsfolk gasp in awe as the colors and movements mesmerize them.

But just as the town's excitement peaks, Pennyworth introduces the cast's nemesis—Mr. Bear, a sly and grumpy bear dressed in a sharp business suit. Mr. Bear represents the volatile nature of the stock market, causing the townsfolk to erupt in laughter.

"Why, if Jack's investments face a series of negative returns in the early years of his retirement, he could run out of money faster than an acrobat soaring through the sky without a net!" Pennyworth exclaims dramatically. The crowd chuckles at the acrobat analogy, appreciating Pennyworth's gift for comedy.

Jack, now wide-eyed and concerned, asks the professor, "But how can I protect myself from this sequence of returns risk, Professor?"

Pennyworth, with a twinkle in his eye, unveils the key to success: diversification. He describes how Jack could balance his investment portfolio by including a mix of stocks, bonds, and other assets to reduce the impact of market volatility. The crowd erupts in applause, thrilled by this wise and whimsical solution.

As the chapter comes to a close, Pennyworth offers practical advice to both Jack and the readers of the book. He explains the importance of staying calm during market downturns and maintaining a disciplined investment strategy. With his humorous expressions and comical gestures, Pennyworth ensures that his valuable advice lands with a chuckle.

In the end, Jack embraces diversification, grateful for the whimsical journey that led him from ignorance to enlightenment. The town of Moneyville buzzes with enthusiasm, armed with newfound knowledge and the ability to dance gracefully through the perils of the Sequence of Returns Risk.

And so, dear readers, this chapter concludes with a joyful reminder: financial planning need not be boring nor intimidating. By allowing colorful characters like Professor Pennyworth and Jack the Jester to guide us through amusing tales, we can learn valuable lessons while sharing a hearty laugh. May you now go forth, armed with wisdom and laughter, and navigate the dance of your own financial futures.

Chapter 31: The Misadventures of Fred the Saver and Ignatius the Impulse Buyer

Once upon a time, in the bustling town of Coinville, lived two characters with starkly different approaches to their finances. They were known far and wide as Fred the Saver and Ignatius the Impulse Buyer. Their contrasting habits made them quite the spectacle to the townsfolk, with Fred always tucked away in the corner of his modest home counting every penny, while Ignatius could be seen parading around town with bags upon bags of unnecessary purchases.

Fred the Saver was a notorious tightwad. He made spreadsheets for everything, from grocery shopping to the air he breathed. "No expense is too small," Fred would say, wearing his frugalness as a badge of honor. Many an evening, he could be found sitting in his rocking chair, meticulously rationing each bite of his humble dinner, and even his neighbors' whispers could not entice him to spend recklessly.

Across the rolling hills, Ignatius the Impulse Buyer lived a life full of extravaganza. His mansion, with its golden gates and a fleet of luxury cars parked outside, was the envy of all who passed by. Ignatius had a soft spot for shiny trinkets, irresistible gadgets, and flamboyant accessories. People even whispered that he owned a closet full of hats, each to match a different pair of shoes. Ignatius believed life was too short to resist the siren song of the latest trends, and embracing his whims brought him an untold amount of joy.

One fine morning, the town crier trumpeted exciting news: a traveling band of musicians would give a free concert in Coinville's grand square! Both Fred and Ignatius, each in their peculiar ways, were thrilled. Fred immediately saw a chance to spend an evening of musical enjoyment without opening his wallet.

"Ignatius, my dear friend," Fred said, leaning towards his neighbor's gleaming gate, "why don't we invite your entire mansion to enjoy this free concert?"

Ignatius whooped with glee, unable to control his impulses. With a flurry of excitement, he sent messengers galloping through town, extending invitations to friends and strangers alike. The entire square was soon buzzing with anticipation.

Meanwhile, Fred plotted a different course. He subtly gathered necessities for the event the coming evening, always choosing the most cost-effective options. He packed a homemade picnic basket with a few tantalizing delicacies and even brought along a homemade pair of binoculars to spot the musicians from afar. Fred believed that saving money was just as important as enjoying the concert itself.

As the sun dipped below the horizon, Coinville's grand square brimmed with expectant townsfolk. Fred and Ignatius found themselves standing side by side, awaiting the musicians' harmonious melodies. The conductor waved her baton, and the music swept through the air, filling every ear.

Fred, with his homemade binoculars, gasped as a harmonica player stepped forward, flawlessly hitting high notes that seemed to defy human capability. Ignatius, however, was so deeply engrossed in his latest purchase – a sparkling cane with bells adorning its handle – that he barely registered the harmonica player's incredible talent.

Night after night, the duo, Fred the Saver and Ignatius the Impulse Buyer, attended various events in town, each with their distinct approach. Fred delighted in his clever budgeting, always managing to have a delightful frugal time. Ignatius, on the other hand, reveled in his extravagant purchases, ending up entangled in a web of empty pockets and credit card debts that followed him like a shadow.

Soon, the final fable unfolded as Ignatius found himself in the grips of financial ruin, surrounded by stacks of unpaid bills. Despite all his shiny trinkets, he realized he had very little to show for his extravagant lifestyle. It was then that his eyes wandered towards Fred, who, with only the simplest of possessions, had found true enjoyment in life.

"Hmm," Ignatius thought to himself, "perhaps I should learn a thing or two from Fred's sensible ways."

And so, Ignatius embarked on a journey of financial self-discovery, seeking out Fred's sage advice and adopting the ways of a saver. With newfound discipline, Ignatius slowly but surely paid off his debts, and his golden gates shone brighter than ever before.

From that day forward, Coinville's townfolk marveled at the transformed Ignatius, who was no longer drowning in shallow purchases but instead splashed in the refreshing waters of savings. Meanwhile, Fred found joy in knowing that his fable had inspired someone to change their ways, proving that even the most contrasting characters could coexist in harmony.

And so, dear reader, the tale of Fred the Saver and Ignatius the

Impulse Buyer reminds us all of the importance of balancing our desires with our needs. As you venture forth on your journey through the financial realm, remember that saving wisely will always be a key ingredient to a life filled with happiness, laughter, and, of course, financial fun.

Chapter 32: The Remarkable Tale of Harry the Hippo and His Hilarious HSA Adventure

Once upon a time, in a lush and lively jungle, there lived a jolly hippopotamus named Harry. Harry loved munching on juicy watermelons, taking refreshing dips in the river, and, of course, rolling in cool mud on scorching summer days. But despite his love for simple pleasures, Harry often found himself in quite a pickle when it came to managing his health. Little did he know that his world was about to be turned upside down by the magical wonders of a Health Savings Account!

One sunny morning, as Harry waddled along the river bank, he stumbled upon a peculiar-looking monkey named Miles. Miles was known for his quirky sense of humor and mysterious knowledge of the jungle's secrets.

"Miles, my good friend!" Harry exclaimed, his big eyes widening with excitement. "Why are you hopping around like a wild monkey on a sugar rush today?"

Miles paused, letting out a mischievous chuckle. "Oh, dear Harry, you won't believe the adventure I've embarked upon! I've discovered a hidden treasure that will solve all your health woes and save you from countless headaches!"

Harry perked up, his ears perking up with curiosity. "Hidden treasure? How does that relate to my health?"

Miles slapped his furry forehead lightly, pretending to be

shocked. "Oh, Harry! Haven't you heard about the mysterious Health Savings Account, the HSA?"

Harry shook his head, looking rather puzzled. "A Health what-now?"

Miles pulled out a shiny golden book from his tail pocket and cleared his throat dramatically. "Behold, Harry! Let me weave a tale of wonder and enlightenment about the magical HSA."

Intrigued, Harry sat down beside Miles, ready to be spellbound by this fable. Little did he know that he was about to embark on an unforgettable journey filled with unexpected twists, turns, and belly laughs.

***

Many moons ago, in a neighboring jungle, lived a wise old elephant named Edward. Now, Edward was astute, but he wasn't too keen on keeping his expenses in check, especially when it came to his health. One day, as he trotted through the jungle with a hefty medical bill in his trunk, he stumbled upon an HSA nestled amongst the foliage.

With a twinkle in his eye, Edward cautiously approached the HSA, like a cheetah sneaking up on its prey. He soon realized the incredible possibilities this magical account held. Little did he know that with an HSA, he could save money for health-related expenses while enjoying some tax savings.

Edward's eyes widened, his wrinkles deepening with anticipation. "An HSA! It's like a pot of gold, hidden in the jungle!"

From that moment on, Edward diligently deposited money into his newfound treasure chest, saving it for medical expenses that might pop up in the future.

Word of the fantastic and practical HSA quickly spread throughout the jungle, reaching lions, giraffes, and even little monkey families. Each hopped, skipped, and jumped to the glorious banks of the HSA, experiencing the wonders it held.

***

"Oh, Miles! The story of Edward the elephant and the HSA is exhilarating!" Harry exclaimed, wiping away tears of laughter. "But, what does this mean for me, an average hippo?"

Miles grinned, his eyes sparkling with mischief. "Oh, Harry, the HSA is not just for the fancy or the mythical creatures of the jungle. It's for everyone, including a comical hippo like yourself."

Harry's heart raced with excitement. The thought of saving money on his medical bills was like discovering a river of watermelons flowing through the jungle. He couldn't wait to dive into the refreshing depths of this magical HSA.

And so, with Miles as his wise and snarky guide, Harry leaped into the world of HSAs, delighting in the newfound power of saving for unexpected medical expenses while enjoying tax benefits. With each new adventure, Harry's confidence in the magical HSA grew, just as his waistline shrank from the cost savings.

From then on, our hero, Harry the Hippo, lived happily ever after, munching watermelons and knowing he had unlocked the secret to managing his health with the help of an HSA.

The end... or rather, the beginning of Harry and his HSA adventures!

Chapter 33: The Wily Fox's Insurance Shenanigans

Once upon a time in the charming village of Moneyville, there lived a sly fox named Felix, known for his sly ways and mischievous nature. Felix was always looking for ways to get ahead, especially when it came to the elaborate game of retirement planning. Retirement, in Felix's mind, equated to endless hours lounging in the luscious grass, sip after sip of elderflower tea, and nary a worry about where the next plate of freshly baked biscuits was coming from.

One sunny morning, as Felix sipped his tea at his favorite café, he overheard a group of retirees chattering animatedly about "living benefits life insurance." Curiosity piqued, Felix eavesdropped shamelessly, abandoning all social graces typical of a fox. He heard tales of how living benefits life insurance could provide a secure financial blanket, with the added perk of withdrawing funds in case of unexpected illnesses or critical injuries – like a bottomless biscuit tin, he thought.

Intrigued by the possibilities, Felix rushed to his den, which was more like an underground mansion complete with a cozy fireplace and imported velvet cushions. He gathered his closest friends – Marty the meerkat, Lola the lynx, and Benny the badger – who, like Felix, were seeking retirement bliss.

Felix dramatically paced the plush carpet of his den as he explained, "My dear friends, imagine a world where retirement planning was as delightful as catching butterflies on a sunny day. I have just unearthed a treasure – living benefits life insurance! It ensures a secure future with the bonus of withdrawing funds for unexpected health emergencies. It's like finding honey-dipped acorns when you least expect them!"

His friends raised their eyebrows, intrigued yet skeptical. "But Felix, isn't life insurance meant for our families in case we leave this world?" Benny queried.

Felix grinned and replied, "Ah, my dear Benny, that's where the brilliance lies! Not only does this living benefits life insurance provide a safety net for our loved ones, but it also allows us to dip into the funds while we're still sprightly! Imagine, a financial boon that protects against both unexpected twists and turns and ensures you can enjoy your golden years to the fullest."

Marty the meerkat scrunched his furry forehead. "Well, Felix, that does sound enticing, but how are we to know if it's worth it? The fine print always seems to be written in the same language they use to confuse us in board meetings."

Felix, with a sly smirk, jumped in, "Ah, my dear friend, I've got that part figured out. You see, the secret to unraveling the mysteries of living benefits life insurance lies in finding a knowledgeable advisor who speaks our language - a fellow woodland creature who'll help us untangle the complexities with charm and wit, just like a master squirrel with a nutcracker."

The friends exchanged glances, their skepticism melting away, replaced by the flickering flames of hope. Lola the lynx, with her keen intuition, summed it up perfectly, "Alright, Felix, you've piqued our interest, and we'll journey with you on this delightful tale of living benefits life insurance. Let's embark on this adventure together and uncover the hidden riches that await."

And so, Felix, Marty, Lola, and Benny set off on their quest, aided by their newfound knowledge and a sprinkle of good fortune. Along the way, they met wild, wacky characters who shared their own tales of success and blunders in the realm of living benefits life insurance. The village of Moneyville became a tapestry of humor, wisdom, and curiosity intertwined, as they learned about the importance of tailored coverage, financial stability, and the true meaning of "living" in living benefits.

With each twist and turn, the friends grew closer, their bonds fortified by laughter and shared moments of unforeseen wisdom. The enchanting tale of their escapades danced across the pages, allowing readers to delve into the whimsical world they created together, all while weaving the golden thread of living benefits life insurance into their very hearts.

In the end, Felix and his friends unlocked the secret to retiring in style with a safety net that doubled as a trampoline for life's unexpected somersaults. The village of Moneyville celebrated their return, heralding them as heroes, champions of wit and wisdom.

And so, dear reader, as Felix and his friends left their mark on Moneyville, they implored you to wander through this whimsical adventure with them, to see that retirement planning need not be a tired march through paperwork and calculations. Instead, through the prism of this comedic fable, you too can discover the charm and advantages of living benefits life insurance – a magical gateway to enjoying your golden years with peace of mind and a twinkle in your eye.

Chapter 34 – Sammy the Squirrel and Ricky the Raccoon's Life Insurance vs Crowd Fundraising

Once upon a time, in the whimsical land of Pennypocket, there lived a witty squirrel named Sammy and a crafty raccoon named Ricky. They were known throughout the land as the kings of mischief and laughter. One bright morning, as they scampered through Meadow Lane, the topic of financial support came up.

"Say, Sammy, have you ever heard of life insurance?" Ricky asked, balancing himself on a tree branch with his bushy tail.

Sammy, collecting acorns with lightning speed, paused for a moment. "Of course, Ricky! It's like a magical shield that ensures your loved ones are cared for when you're no longer around—financial security in the forest, you might say."

Ricky grinned, his eyes gleaming mischievously. "Ah, yes, but have you heard about this newfangled thing called crowd fundraising?"

Sammy looked up, acorns tumbling from his paws. "Crowd fundraising? What on earth is that?"

Ricky twirled his tail excitedly. "Well, Sammy, it's like a grand forest party where all the animals gather to support their fellow creatures. They contribute small amounts of acorns or sticks to raise a large sum. It's like a treasure hunt for charity!"

Sammy's eyes sparkled with curiosity. "Sounds like a fantastic way to help those in need! But let's take a closer look, shall we?"

And so, the two friends set off on an adventure to explore the pros and cons of life insurance and crowd fundraising. Their first stop was the eccentric Wizard of Wisdom, perched in his mystical library atop Oakridge Tower.

"Good day, good day," said the Wizard, his long white beard tickling the pages of his books. "Let me show you the magical pros and cons tables!"

With a flick of his wand, Sammy and Ricky found themselves surrounded by floating tables with words dancing around them.

"Behold, the pros of life insurance!" the Wizard proclaimed.

The table before them burst to life with shiny acorns, tickling their noses with their glittering presence. Sammy and Ricky giggled in delight.

"Life insurance provides security to your family, even if you are no longer around," Ricky read aloud, his voice crackling with excitement.

"And crowd fundraising, though it lacks the magical shield, taps into the generosity of many woodland friends. It brings the community together!" Sammy added, his eyes widening with admiration.

As the Wizard waved his wand once again, the tables transformed into towering columns of cons.

"Ah, the cons," said the Wizard, his voice turning somber. "With life insurance, you must pay premiums regularly. And let us not forget the complex paperwork that can confuse an owl!"

Sammy and Ricky exchanged concerned glances. Then they turned their attention to the next column.

"With crowd fundraising," Ricky read aloud, "there's no guarantee you'll raise the required sum. And sometimes, the cacophony of different voices can make it tough to reach your goal!"

As the tables and columns disappeared, Sammy and Ricky thanked the Wizard for sharing his wisdom.

"Methinks it's time for some real-life examples," whispered Sammy, his eyes brimming with mischief.

And so, the duo embarked on their next adventure—a mission to witness life insurance in action and attend a crowd fundraiser.

They encountered a wise old owl, Professor Featherwing, who had safeguarded his family's future with life insurance. His chicks were happily engaging in acrobatics, cheered on by their friends. Sammy and Ricky joined in, swinging from branches and flipping acorns in the air—all in the name of financial security.

Then, they darted off to a splendid crowd fundraiser held by the bubbly Bunny Brigade. They bounced with joy as animals contributed all sorts of nuts, sticks, and shiny treasures to help a turtle with a broken shell. It was like a carnival in the forest, filled with laughter, admiration, and endless acorns.

As Sammy and Ricky scampered back to their treehouse, they

reflected on their magical journey. They realized that life insurance brought certainty, while crowd fundraising brought unity and a sense of belonging.

"Isn't it marvelous, Ricky?" Sammy exclaimed.

"It surely is, Sammy," Ricky replied, grinning from ear to ear. "Both life insurance and crowd fundraising have their own charm, and each provides unique benefits to those in need."

And so, the squirrel and raccoon lived happily ever after, their mischievous hearts still yearning for laughter and adventure. But whenever the topic of financial support came up, they'd fondly remember the lessons they learned on that delightful day in Pennypocket—the day they discovered the wonders of life insurance and the power of crowd fundraising.

Chapter 35: The Insurance Showdown: Whole Life. Index Universal Life

In the quaint town Valuetown, there lived two friends, Oscar the Owl and Larry the Lizard. One evening, as they sat in their favorite tree at the town's pub, The Financial Nest, an animated discussion broke out amongst the patrons about retirement planning. Eavesdropping on their conversation, Oscar and Larry couldn't resist joining in to bring their unique perspectives to the debate.

The pub echoed with mixed opinions, but one point was clear: everyone wanted financial security in their old age. Oscar, the wise owl, championed the merits of Whole Life Insurance, while Larry, the witty lizard, ardently defended Index Universal Life Insurance (IUL).

With a twinkle in his eye, Oscar began, "Listen, dear friends, Whole Life Insurance offers a lifetime of guarantees. It's like having a cozy nest, nestling you comfortably even during the harshest of storms. The premiums you put in today grow over time and accumulate cash value, providing a secure financial cushion for your retirement."

Larry shot back a witty retort, "Ah, my venerable friend, but have you considered the possibility of attaining higher returns with an IUL? It's like a tree with branches in several markets, agile as a lizard, adapting to changing market conditions. With an IUL, you have the potential for growth tied to an index, plus the added benefit of having a death benefit."

Oscar, raising his feathery eyebrow, countered, "That may be true, but Whole Life Insurance provides a guaranteed cash value growth, even if the market decides to hit rock bottom. It's like eating a delicious worm every day, regardless of how many tasty insects the forest offers."

Larry smirked and replied, "Ah, Oscar, my dear philosopher, but an IUL offers you the chance to capture market gains and still have a minimum guaranteed interest rate, like enjoying a bountiful feast with a dessert buffet. Even if the market is having a party, you're still guaranteed a slice of cake."

Their banter continued late into the night as the pub patrons chuckled and enjoyed the lively debate. Each character introduced an insurance salesman sidekick trying to sway the other to their point of view.

Enter Jerry the Jaguar, a suave Whole Life Insurance salesman with a perfectly coiffed mane. "Ah, Oscar, my friend, imagine the serenity of knowing your policy won't lapse even if you encounter financial troubles. It's like having a caretaker watching over your financial wellbeing, ready to bail you out if you ever experience hard times."

Not to be outdone, Lucy the Llama, an energetic IUL saleswoman with a perpetual smile, debonairly emerged, and quipped, "Larry, my good sir, picture the flexibility of IUL, like a tightrope walker jumping from one market potential to another, harnessing all the excitement of financial growth."

As Oscar and Larry listened to the persuasive arguments, they both realized that these insurance have their pros and cons. They could see the forest through the trees, recognizing that different financial goals necessitated different solutions.

In the end, the two embraced, deciding not to choose sides but to fashion their own unique retirement plans, blending the advantages of both Whole Life and IUL. They laughed and toasted, sipping colorful cocktails named "Protection Punch" and "Growth Gimlet." So, dear reader, the lesson of the story is clear: when it comes to retirement planning consider all options, understand the pros and cons, and create a personalized plan that suits your goals. The journey to financial security is not about choosing a side but navigating the vast insurance landscape while savoring the enjoyable debate and the camaraderie along the way.

Chapter 36: The Curious Tale of Worry Wolf and Smarty Squirrel

Once a time, in the sunny meadows of Moneyville, there lived an anxious and cautious wolf named Worrywart. Now don't be fooled by his fierce appearance; Worrywart had a heart of gold but a mind full of doubts. He always worried about his future and how to provide for his family.

Enter Smarty Squirrel, an intelligent and astute resident of Moneyville. Smarty had an uncanny ability to crack complex financial conundrums and was often seen burrowing through piles of books in his cozy oak tree.

One fine day, as Worrywart was aimlessly pacing the meadow, he crossed paths with Smarty. Curiosity piqued, Worrywart summoned the courage to approach Smarty.

"Excuse me, dear Smarty," Worrywart hesitantly began. "I can't help but fret about the best way to secure a prosperous future for my little wolf cubs. What would you suggest?"

Smarty Squirrel, with a playful twinkle in his eyes, replied, "Ah, dear Worrywart, fret not! I have two tales for you, each starring a financial strategy that may set your worries at bay. Sit back, listen, and let your whiskers tingle with awe!"

Worrrywarrt settled down, his ears perked with anticipation.

"The first tale is that of the delightful 529 plan," Smarty announced gleefully. "Imagine a magical pot where you can stash money away for your cub's education. It grows and grows over time, just like a beanstalk! The best part is that it grows tax-free, and when your cubs are ready for higher education, those golden funds can be withdrawn without any taxes."

Worrywart's eyes widened. "Oh, Smarty! That sounds marvelous! But what if my cubs decide not to pursue higher education? Will all those golden beans go to waste?"

Smarty smiled knowingly. "Fear not, dear Worrywart! With a 529 plan, you can transfer the funds to another family member, like a cousin or an aunt. Alternatively, you could even use the money to invest in a small business venture. Simply splendid, isn't it?"

Worrywart's worries began to melt away, as he envisioned a world of possibilities for his cubs. "But Smarty," he interrupted, "what about this Index Universal Life insurance thingy I've heard about? Can it help secure a prosperous future too?"

Smarty nodded and prepared his second tale. "Ah, the remarkable tale of IUL, my dear Worrywart! Picture this: an insurance policy that not only offers a death benefit to protect your loved ones, but also accumulates cash value over time. This cash value is tied to an index, like the S&P 500, and grows as the index cherishes with time."

Worrywart's tail wagged with excitement. "Cash value, you say? So, could I use it to finance my cubs' college education?"

Smarty smirked. "Indeed! In the enchanted realm of IUL, you can access the cash value to fund their academic adventures. It even offers a safety net, with some policies guaranteeing a minimum return even if the index falters. Isn't that marvelous?"

Worrywart couldn't help but feel torn. The 529 plan dazzled him with its tax-free growth, while IUL mesmerized him with its flexible cash value and safety net.

"But Smarty," Worrywart whined, "how can I know which path to pursue? Which tale should guide my financial destiny?"

Smarty Squirrel crossed his arms, his face mimicking an ancient financial sage. "Ah, Worrywart, a question that goes to the core of our tale. The key lies in understanding your financial goals, your risk appetite, and the magical whims of the market. Speak with financial wizards who can guide you through the forest of options. Only then will you uncover the path that leads to your financial happily ever after!"

Worrywart nodded, his head filled with enlightenment. "Thank you, Smarty Squirrel, for sharing these marvelous tales. I shall embark on a quest to learn more, make informed decisions, and secure a prosperous future for my little wolf cubs!"

And with that, Worrywart trotted away, his paws brimming with newfound confidence. As for Smarty Squirrel, he smiled and retreated to his cozy oak tree, ready to guide the next befuddled soul in the tangled financial forest of Moneyville.

The moral of the tale? Whether you choose the enchanting 529 or the mesmerizing IUL, it's wise to gather all the knowledge, seek guidance, and make decisions informed by your unique financial situation.

And so, dear reader, go forth, learn, and write your own financial tale with a happy ending. The enchanted forest of Moneyville awaits your curious spirit!

Chapter 37: The Duel of Dough and Honey - The Bitter-Sweet Battle between Roth and IULs

Once upon a time, in the enchanting land of Financeville, there lived two fearless and completely opposite warriors. Dough, a jolly, rotund character, was the knight representing the mighty Roth products. In contrast, Honey, an agile and mysterious figure, championed the cause of the bewitching IULs (Indexed Universal Life Insurance) with living benefits.

The story of their intense rivalry spread far and wide throughout the kingdom, and the people became divided on which warrior was the true hero. To settle the dispute once and for all, the royal council organized an epic debate. The audience gathered, their hearts pounding with anticipation.

Dough, as the defender of Roth products, began with a grand flourish, "Ladies and gentlemen, imagine a world where you have complete control over your money! With Roth, you pay taxes upfront, like a responsible citizen, but once you've done so, you never pay taxes again! Never!"

The crowd gasped in awe as Dough continued his animated speech, gesticulating wildly. "Think about the future, dear friends With Roth, your investments grow tax-free, and when it's time to retire all the money is yours to spend without worrying about Uncle Sam!"

Honey, the IUL avenger, could not bear to remain silent. "Ah, my dear audience, let me weave a tale of financial wonderment!

With IULs, you blend the eternal power of insurance with the radiant beauty of investment growth. It's a mysterious dance of protection and prosperity!"

The crowd leaned forward, captivated by Honey's silky voice. "Picture this: your money soars with the market, yet never falls with market tumbles! And if life throws lemons at you, fear not! IULs with living benefits can provide protection and an income stream if you become critically ill or injured. Sweet, succulent honey, just a sip away!"

Dough wrinkled his forehead, skeptical of Honey's words. "But tell me, mysterious magician, are there drawbacks? Surely, no financial product is without its flaws."

Honey smiled, revealing a set of perfectly white teeth. "Indeed, dear Dough; IULs have their complexities. The returns may not always match the market's glory, for the forces that dictate them are ever-shifting. This dance can confuse even the most astute investors, and high surrender charges can tie one's hands if withdrawal is necessary."

Dough chuckled smugly, confident in his chances of victory. "Ah, Honey, you do speak the language of challenges! But when it comes to Roth, the disadvantages are few and far between. Some lament its contribution limits, shackling the mightiest of savers. Others thirst for the taste of a juicy tax deduction, stolen forever by Roth's upfront taxation!"

The audience giggled at the comedic exchange unfolding before them. The energy in the room intensified.

The royal judge rose from his seat, a wise expression guiding his every word. "Ladies and gentlemen, the battle of Roth versus IULs may seem like an epic duel, but the answer lies in your needs and personal situation."

Dough and Honey, side by side, stood in unison, showing a united front. "In truth, dear readers, both Roth products and IULs can be valuable assets in your financial journey. Their complexities and implications make them powerful allies, but also formidable foes."

As the crowd erupted into applause, the knights representing Roth and IULs embraced, their rivalry abandoned in the face of a more significant truth. They whispered in unison, "Remember, dear citizens, seek the counsel of a wise financial advisor, for they possess the knowledge to navigate the complexities and unleash the true potential of these financial wonders!"

The curtains closed, the applause fading into the distance, leaving the audience in awe of the enlightening, humorous adventure they had just experienced.

And so, the fable of Roth and IULs taught the people of Financeville that financial products, like life itself, are never as simple as they seem. But armed with knowledge, a sprinkle of humor, and the guidance of experts, one can conquer the complexities and embrace the infinite possibilities that lie in the realm of finance.

Chapter 38: The Tale of Prudence and Rollo—The Wise Squirrel and the Mischievous Raccoon

Amidst the sprawling woodland, where the trees whispered secrets to the dancing leaves, lived two creatures with a penchant for financial planning—the wise squirrel, Prudence, and the mischievous raccoon, Rollo.

Prudence was known throughout the forest as a master of saving acorns for the future. She always made wise choices, preparing for seasons when the nuts were scarce. Rollo, on the other hand, was notorious for gobbling up his acorns on the spot. The concept of saving and planning for the unknown seemed entirely foreign to him.

One fine morning, as Prudence sat atop a mossy rock, carefully counting her acorns, Rollo bounded towards her, furiously eyeing the small treasure. With a mischievous grin, he jeered, "Prudence, my friend, why hoard all those acorns? Enjoy them now, while we're still young and spry!"

Prudence, donning her wise smile, replied, "Ah, Rollo, you see, acorns are like money. If you spend them all now, what will you have in the leaner times, when the trees bear no fruit?"

Rollo recoiled in disbelief. "But Prudence, have you gone nuts? What's the difference between your acorns and mine?"

Prudence leaped off the rock, tail swinging with purpose. "Ah, my dear Rollo, let me enlighten you. You see, my acorns are akin to Roth products, while yours represent pre-tax products."

Rollo scratched his head, perplexed. "Roth and pre-tax? Who are they? More acorns?"

Prudence chuckled, her eyes twinkling with excitement. "No, no, my friend! Roth and pre-tax are different ways to save for the future. With Roth products, you pay taxes upfront, but when you withdraw the money in retirement, no taxes are due! It's like eating acorns without worrying about counting them later."

Rollo's eyes widened in comprehension, "So, it's like having an acorn feast without a single stomachache?"

Prudence nodded with pride, "Precisely, dear Rollo. On the other hand, pre-tax products allow you to delay paying taxes until you withdraw the money in retirement. It's like gorging on acorns now and tallying up your bills later."

Rollo grinned, his paws rubbing together. "I do enjoy the taste of acorns without thinking about consequences!"

Prudence tapped her foot gently, her eyes filled with wisdom. "But, Rollo, my friend, by paying taxes upfront through Roth products, you ensure that your acorns will grow larger without being nibbled away by taxes. It's like the tree's branches spreading wider and heavier with luscious fruit."

Rollo scratched his head again, his eyes widening in amazement. "So, you're telling me that paying taxes now leads to bigger acorns later?"

Prudence nodded approvingly. "Yes, indeed, Rollo. By choosing the right savings approach, we can grow our acorns without worrying about the tax monster sneaking up on us."

Rollo chuckled, his mischievousness now paired with newfound understanding. "Well, Prudence, my friend, I guess there's more to acorns than meets the eye. Perhaps it's time I start thinking about my future nut-needs too!"

Prudence beamed, placing one tiny paw on Rollo's shoulder. "I'm glad you see the light, Rollo. Now, let's journey together and explore the importance of wise financial planning, so we can both enjoy a prosperous and acorn-filled future!"

And so, with a spring in their steps and laughter in their hearts, Prudence and Rollo set forth on an adventure through the woodland, spreading financial wisdom and acorn-saving know-how to all the critters they met along the way.

And thus, dear readers, remember the tale of Prudence and Rollo, and embrace the knowledge that planning for the future, just like saving acorns, can yield great rewards in the end.

Chapter 39: 401k vs Roth 401k - The Battle of the Retirement Plans

Once upon a time, in the bustling town of Financialville, a friendly squirrel named Sam and a wise old owl named Oliver were strolling through the forest, engaged in their favorite pastime – Hilarious Financial Fables, of course!

As they settled down on a comfy tree branch, Sam exclaimed, "Oliver, my friend, I've heard a tale about two mysterious creatures, 401k, and Roth 401k. Can you enlighten me about their differences?"

Oliver, with a twinkle in his eyes, began his whimsical tale.

"Ah, Sam, let me introduce you to Mr. 401k, a traditional fellow who likes to postpone his taxes. Mr. 401k is like a sneak attack on Uncle Sam's pockets. Employees contribute to him from their pre-tax income, making it possible to invest more without paying any taxes upfront. It's like enjoying a scrumptious dinner without the bill spoiling the mood."

Intrigued, Sam interjected, "But what's the catch? There's always a catch!"

Oliver nodded sagely. "Indeed, my friend. Mr. 401k has a cunning side. When the time comes for withdrawals, Uncle Sam's greed awakens. You must pay taxes on the money you take out, and if you withdraw before you're 59 and a half, he even slaps you with a 10% penalty! It's like getting peanuts for dinner and then losing them to a pesky bandit!"

Sam chuckled at the mental image of a squirrel losing peanuts to a bandit and prompted Oliver to continue. "And what about the mysterious Roth 401k, Oliver? Is he a worthy adversary?"

Oliver chuckled heartily. "Oh, my friend, he surely is! Let me introduce you to Mr. Roth 401k, the unbelievably tax-free squirrel of retirement plans. With Roth 401k, employees pay taxes on their contributions upfront, and once Uncle Sam gets his cut, the money grows tax-free like a magical beanstalk! And the best part? When retirement day arrives, the withdrawals are completely tax-free! It's like devouring a never-ending supply of nuts that miraculously regenerate!"

Sam's eyes widened with wonder. "That sounds amazing! So, no pesky penalties or hidden costs?"

Oliver smiled. "Well, not exactly, dear Sam. Mr. Roth 401k doesn't appreciate it if you withdraw earnings before five years have passed since your first contribution or if you're under 59 and a half. In such cases, Uncle Sam might seize a portion of your goodies as a penalty. It's like finding out your magically regenerating nuts have a delay in regeneration, leaving you with a rumbling tummy for a while!"

Sam laughed heartily at the thought of a squirrely tummy rumbling, and then he turned serious. "So, Oliver, which one do you recommend?"

Oliver stroked his wise old feathers and replied, "Ah, that, my friend, depends on your current financial situation and your appetite for future taxes. If you believe your tax rates will be higher in the future, then the Roth 401k might be your acorn of choice. But if you want immediate tax savings and assume your tax rates will be lower in retirement, then Mr. 401k is your nutty buddy."

Sam scratched his furry chin, contemplating his decision. "Thank you, Oliver! With your amusing fable, I'm better prepared to choose between 401k and Roth 401k. Now, let's find those magically regenerating nuts, shall we?"

With that, the two friends scampered off through the forest, laughing and chattering like a couple of true financial fable enthusiasts.

So, remember, dear reader, when it comes to choosing between 401k and Roth 401k, consider your current situation, and your expectations for the future, and most importantly, never underestimate the power of a hilarious fable to make even the most complex financial matters digestible. Happy investing, and may your retirement days be filled with laughter and abundant nuts!

Chapter 40: The Misadventures of Mr. Paddlesworth and the 401(k) Monster

Once upon a time, in the quaint little town of Savvyville, lived a well-to-do family named the Paddlesworths. Mr. Paddlesworth, a portly and perpetually anxious man, was always perplexed about planning for his retirement. One day, he happened upon a captivating seminar on the power of 401(k)s. The speaker, a silver-haired financial wizard, promised great fortune and a golden future to anyone who followed his advice.

Excited and dreaming of riches, Mr. Paddlesworth returned home and eagerly shared the news with his wife, Mrs. Paddlesworth. "My dearest, I've just learned about this magical creature called the 401(k)!" he exclaimed, waving a brochure that read 'Retire in Paradise.' "It has the power to grow our money exponentially and whisk us away to a life of luxury!"

Mrs. Paddlesworth raised an eyebrow. "Exponentially, you say? Well, that does sound intriguing, my dear. But are we putting all our eggs in one basket? What if this creature turns out to be a monster?"

"Nonsense, my love!" Mr. Paddlesworth scoffed, his eyes gleaming with dollar signs. "This expert assured me that a 401(k) is the only friend we need for our retirement."

And so, our intrepid couple embarked on a journey with their newfound friend, the 401(k). Little did they know, this beast had a voracious appetite for unprepared souls.

Months passed, and the Paddlesworths diligently fed their 401(k) monster, sacrificing their daily lattes and family vacations to appease its insatiable appetite. But one gloomy Sunday afternoon, disaster struck. The stock market hiccuped, causing the 401(k) monster to growleth and lose its charm, devouring their wealth faster than Mrs. Paddlesworth could say, "I told you so."

Desperate, they reached out to a wise old sage named Simon, a wizened financial guru known for his wit. "Ah, the perils of relying solely on the 401(k) monster," Simon mused, stroking his beard. "It has an insidious charm, does it not?"

Simon carefully elucidated the couple on the danger of putting all their retirement eggs in one monstrous basket. He regaled them with tales of market crashes, corporate scandals, and the treacherous beast known as inflation.

"Mr. Paddlesworth, have you considered diversification?" Simon quizzed, his eyes twinkling with wisdom.

"Diversification?" cried Mr. Paddlesworth, his brow furrowing. "What monstrous gibberish is that?"

Simon chuckled, revealing a smile that could put Cheshire cats to shame. "Imagine investing your money in different creatures—maybe a fearsome dragon called real estate, a trusty steed named index funds, or maybe even a gleaming knight dressed in bonds."

Mr. Paddlesworth's eyes widened as he beheld the wisdom in Simon's words. "Oh, the folly of my ways!" he lamented, smacking his palm against his forehead. "I've been so foolish, casting all my hopes on one capricious creature!"

Simon reassured the couple that all was not lost, leaving them with sage advice. "Fear not, dear Paddlesworths, for it is never too late to diversify! Seek guidance from a knight-of-all-trades financial advisor who can help you build a retirement army. Remember, a comic tragedy can be a delightful marvel when you embrace diversity!"

With newfound resolve, the Paddlesworths bid farewell to their 401(k) monster, charting a course toward a diverse retirement portfolio. From that day forward, they lived a life of prosperity and adventure, learning the valuable lesson that planning for retirement should never be trusted to a single mythological creature.

And so, dear readers, take heed from the misadventures of Mr. Paddlesworth and his pursuit of a golden future. Let them be a cautionary tale, reminding you to diversify your retirement plans, seek advice from wise sages like Simon, and always be prepared for the perils and pitfalls that lie in waiting on your financial journey.

Chapter 41: The Magician's Mirage

Once upon a time in the bustling town of Moneyville, there lived a group of eager workers, each striving for a prosperous retirement. Among them was Reggie the Rabbit, an enthusiastic young employee with dreams of early retirement. Reggie had heard whispers of a magical tool known as "retirement matching programs," which promised a way to effortlessly double one's savings. Intrigued, Reggie set out to uncover the truth behind this enchanting prospect.

On a sunny Monday morning, Reggie skipped joyfully into the office, clutching a printout of a shiny new retirement matching program leaflet. As his coworkers buzzed around him, Reggie exclaimed, "Fellow employees, listen up! We've been missing out on something incredible! This retirement matching program is like a golden ticket to unlimited wealth!"

The office chatter stopped as everyone gathered around Reggie, their eyes wide with curiosity.

"Reggie, tell us more about this mysterious program!" said Patty Pig, her snout twitching with excitement.

With a mischievous grin, Reggie began his tale. "Word has it that the company, in its unmatched generosity, has agreed to contribute a certain percentage of each employee's salary to their retirement accounts. Yes, you heard me right, folks. Free money!"

The room erupted in cheers and applause, with the sweet melody of dollar signs jingling in their heads. But amidst the revelry, a wise old owl named Oliver quietly approached Reggie.

"Young Reggie," Oliver said, raising an all-knowing wing, "Remember, the path to financial security is strewn with illusions. Before you journey any further, I advise you to seek a wider perspective."

Puzzled, Reggie asked, "But Oliver, how can there be any catch when it's free money from the company?"

Oliver chuckled, his feathers shimmering with wisdom. "Ah, my dear Reggie, nothing in this world is truly free. Retirement matching programs might appear miraculous, but they often disguise the risks of relying solely on them."

Reggie's eyes widened; his curiosity piqued. "Tell me more, Oliver! I want to uncover the secrets behind this enchanting mirage."

With an approving nod, Oliver unfurled his wings and began:

"In the land of Moneyville, there once lived a mesmerizing magician by the name of Matcho. Matcho had long captivated the townspeople, luring them into his mesmerizing act of offering free money. One day, a young squirrel named Sammy, enticed by Matcho's promises, placed all his savings into the magician's hands, relying entirely on Matcho's magic for his future."

Reggie leaned in, hanging on Oliver's every word.

"But as Sammy approached his retirement age, Matcho's magic started to fade. The funds accumulated from the retirement matching program were restricted, tied up in specific investments and subject to taxes and high management fees. Sammy realized too late that the promised free money wasn't so free after all."

Reggie gasped in disbelief. "So, what can we do, Oliver? Is there no hope for financial security?"

Oliver smiled warmly. "Fear not, young Reggie. All is not lost! Like a clever hare, you must diversify your financial strategies. While the retirement matching program can be a helpful tool, it should not be your sole focus. Invest your savings wisely, exploring a range of avenues such as stocks, bonds, and real estate. And don't forget the magic word: compounding. Start saving early and let time work its charm."

Reggie sighed with relief, feeling enlightened and eager to confront the challenges ahead. "Thank you, Oliver, for showing me the truth behind the mirage. I won't fall prey to the fallacy of 'free money.'"

As Reggie left, beaming with newfound knowledge, the rest of the office began to disperse, each deep in thought. Oliver, the wise old owl, watched over them, confident that his story had planted a seed of financial wisdom.

And so, dear readers, let Reggie's journey serve as a reminder that while retirement matching programs can act as a valuable tool, supplementing them wisely with diversified financial strategies is the key to a secure and comfortable retirement. As we navigate the winding path to financial freedom, let us always remember the enchanting words of Oliver: "Nothing in this world is truly free."

Chapter 42 – The Legendary Tales of 401(k): Making Sense of Retirement Accounts as You Bid Farwell to Your Job

Once upon a time in the bustling town of Financeville there lived a clever squirrel named Sammy. Sammy spent his days scurrying around, hiding acorns and saving for his retirement in his trusty 401k account. One sunny morning, as he hastily darted towards the bank (which happened to be a tree stump), he met his dear friend, Bernard the Bear.

"Good morning, Sammy! I noticed you're in quite a hurry," said Bernard, a big grin spreading across his furry face.

Sammy stopped and caught his breath. "Ah, Bernard! You won't believe it! I'm about to embark on a great adventure, leaving my current job, and I'm not sure what to do with my 401k!"

Bernard's eyes widened, intrigued. "Oh, Sammy, this is a challenging decision indeed! Let me tell you a tale of what happened to my cousin, Barry the Bear, when he found himself in a similar predicament."

Sammy's ears perked up. "Oh, please do tell, Bernard!"

So Bernard began his cautionary tale. "Once upon a time, Barry left his job and wanted to take his 401k with him. He decided to cash it out, thinking it would be like finding a pot of honey at the end of the rainbow. But alas, the taxman came knocking, and poor Barry ended up paying a hefty penalty."

Sammy gasped. "Oh, no! That's not what I want to happen to me!"

Bernard nodded sympathetically. "Indeed, Sammy, it was a sticky situation. But fear not, for there is a better way! When you leave your job, you have a few options, and one of the smartest choices is to roll your 401k into an IRA."

Sammy scratched his head. "IRA? Is that a cousin of yours, Bernard?"

Bernard chuckled. "No, Sammy, an IRA stands for Individual Retirement Account. It's a special account designed for retirement savings. Rolling your 401k into an IRA allows you to keep your savings growing tax-deferred, just like a delicious acorn in your secret stash."

Sammy's eyes lit up. "That sounds fantastic, Bernard! But how do I get an IRA?"

Bernard put his paw on Sammy's shoulder. "Ah, my curious friend, you can set up an IRA with an online broker or a financial advisor. They'll guide you through the process, just like a wise old owl showing you the way in the dark of the night."

Sammy's tail wagged with excitement. "Thank you, Bernard! You've saved me from a sticky situation. I shall roll my 401k into an IRA and keep those acorns growing safely."

Bernard grinned. "You're welcome, Sammy! It wouldn't be a fable without a happy ending, now would it?"

As Sammy scampered off to secure his financial future, Bernard called after him, "And remember, Sammy, don't forget to rebalance your portfolio from time to time. Diversify like a clever chameleon changing colors to match its surroundings!"

And so, Sammy learned an important lesson that day – to be smart in managing his 401k when leaving a job. He rolled his savings into an IRA, avoided unnecessary penalties, and lived happily ever after, enjoying his golden years filled with acorns aplenty.

The end.

Chapter 43: The Tax Bracket Shuffle

Once upon a time in the land of Retirenia, a charming village called Tinypurse was known for its hardworking inhabitants and their deep-rooted fear of taxes. In this quaint village lived a diligent squirrel named Sid, and a wise old owl named Winston. Though they were lifelong friends, Sid and Winston had differing opinions about taxes and their impact on retirement.

Sid believed that retiring meant a life of financial ease and lower taxes. He dreamed of lounging under a coconut tree without a care in the world, convinced that his retirement nest egg was secure. Winston, on the other hand, was a bit of a nerd and had spent his days studying tax codes and retirement funds. He knew a secret that many in Tinypurse overlooked - the myth of being in a lower tax bracket in retirement.

One sunny day, Sid and Winston met at the Tinypurse café, famous for its acorn coffee and nutty pastries. Winston sipped his steaming acorn brew while Sid sipped his concoction of pine cone tea mixed with caramel. As they were savoring their drinks, a group of lively retirees approached their table.

The retirees were famous in Tinypurse for their extravagant lifestyles and tales of exotic vacations. Leading the pack was the confident rabbit, Roger, holding up a mysterious golden key.

"Guess what, pals?" Roger exclaimed, a mischievous glint in his eyes. "This key represents a life of endless luxury, and it can all be yours if you retire early and stay in a lower tax bracket."

Sid's eyes widened with excitement, while Winston rolled his eyes and skeptically scratched his feathery forehead. Aware of his friend's peculiar interest in tax matters, Sid turned toward Winston. "Tell me, wise old owl, what say you about this golden key?"

Winston peered at the golden key and replied, "Ah, my friends, the allure of lower taxes in retirement is a sly myth. It's like winning a lottery ticket without knowing the prize. Tax brackets are not as straightforward as they seem."

Intrigued, the retirees leaned in closer to listen to Winston's wise words.

"Imagine the land of taxes as an enormous staircase," Winston began, using his wings to illustrate his point in the air. "Each step represents a different tax bracket, and as you climb up the staircase, your income increases, leading to higher taxes."

Sid interjected, "But doesn't retiring mean you earn less, and therefore you're in a lower tax bracket?"

Winston raised an eyebrow and smiled. "Ah, my dear squirrel, it's not that simple. Once you retire, your sources of income change. Now, instead of a monthly salary, you'll have various revenue streams, such as Social Security, retirement accounts, and possibly income from investments."

Sid's face sank as he realized he hadn't considered those factors. He glanced at the key in Roger's paw, no longer believing it held the key to a lower tax bracket.

"But wait, there's more," Winston continued with a twinkle in his eye. "As retirees, you might also receive money from your

144

pensions or take withdrawals from your retirement accounts. These financial boosts can lead you to climb up the tax staircase, leaving you in a higher tax bracket than you anticipated."

Roger gasped, realizing his golden key was losing its luster. "So, you're saying that retiring with a lower tax bracket is not guaranteed?" he asked, his ears drooping.

Winston nodded, adding, "Indeed. Retirement is a time to be smart about tax strategies. It's crucial to consider income sources, deductions, timing, and to seek professional advice. Only then can you craft a plan suited for your unique circumstances."

Sid turned to Roger and the other retirees, a newfound determination in his eyes. "Let's not be fooled by this myth, my friends. Knowledge is our true golden key! We must educate ourselves and be proactive in understanding and planning our finances."

The retirees listened intently, their hopes rekindled. They realized that retirement wasn't all about lazing under coconut trees, but about making informed choices and adapting to the ever-changing tax landscape.

As they left the café, Sid and Winston exchanged a knowing glance. They understood that although taxes may not be the most glamorous topic, it was essential to grasp their complexities. Armed with newfound knowledge and their friendship intact, Sid and Winston embarked on a mission to debunk more myths in Tinypurse and beyond.

And so, the village of Tinypurse became a hub of tax-savvy retirees, forever grateful for the wisdom of Winston and their friend, Sid. From that day forward, they laughed, learned, and challenged the misconceptions surrounding tax brackets in retirement, one fable at a time.

The end... or rather, the beginning of enlightened retirement planning in Tinypurse!

Chapter 44: "Money in the Mermaid's Hands... and Beyond!"

As the sun set on the city skyline, the eccentric billionaire Sebastian "Penny" Pinchman gathered all the main characters of "Financial Fun" at his lavish penthouse for an extravagant dinner party. The chaos that had unfolded throughout the book had left all of them with a rollercoaster of emotions, but now was the time for resolution and laughter.

Penny, sporting a top hat and a monocle, raised his glass of champagne and addressed the curious crowd, "Ladies and gentlemen, I thank you all for being here tonight. It's time to celebrate the end of our tangled financial web and the friendships formed along the way."

The group, expecting a somber affair, glanced at each other, bewildered but intrigued. Penny winked mischievously and continued, "But before we proceed, I have one final surprise for you all. Feast your eyes on my latest invention, the 'Money Mermaid'!"

With a dramatic flourish, Penny unveiled an elaborate fish tank on the table, inside of which was a fully animated and talking mermaid. The mermaid had a pile of gold coins balanced on her shimmering tail, sparkling pearls adorning her hair, and a voice that oozed innocence.

"I am Serena the Money Mermaid, here to grant one final wish to each of our wonderful friends!" Serena declared, winking at the confused and excited group.

First, Penny's loyal assistant, Oliver, couldn't resist. "I wish for a never-ending supply of the world's finest macaroni and cheese!"

As if on cue, mac and cheese started pouring out from the bookshelves, the ceilings, the windows, and even from Serena's magical fish tank. Everyone laughed and dived into their cheesy delight.

Next, the ambitious banker, Victoria, sheepishly put forth her wish. "I wish to transform all the money stolen from innocent victims back into their rightful hands."

Suddenly, the penthouse was filled with a symphony of ringing cell phones and email notifications as the restored funds flooded back into the accounts of those who had been swindled. The room erupted with relieved laughter and grateful applause.

Anita, the tough-as-nails stock trader, leaned forward with a mischievous smile. "I wish for a never-ending supply of comfy slippers to keep my feet cozy as I conquer the market!"

To her surprise, slippers of every color and style rained down from the ceiling, causing everyone to laugh and slip them on, forming a chaotic slipper fashion show.

Finally, the charismatic gambler, Max, spoke up. "I wish to be the world's luckiest man, able to win at anything I desire."

With an uproarious cheer from the group, Max was transformed into a four-leaf clover himself. Everywhere he went, objects fell into his lap, from winning lottery tickets to the sudden inheritance of a candy factory. Laughs echoed throughout the penthouse as Max shared his newfound luck by showering his friends with silly gifts.

Amid the mayhem and laughter, Penny clinked his glass, demanding attention once more. "Now, my esteemed friends, let's never forget the valuable lessons we've learned. Money is merely a means to happiness, and true wealth lies in our relationships and the laughter we share."

As the hilarity continued, the characters danced and reveled in their newfound closure and camaraderie. They realized that despite their Financial Fun, they had emerged stronger and happier than ever before.

And so, the final pages of "Fractured Financial Tales" closed with uproarious laughter, misplaced slippers, and a quirky billionaire who taught them that sometimes, the best currency in life is the comedy and joy that accompanies the most unexpected twists and turns.

The end.

www.ingramcontent.com/pod-product-compliance
Lightning Source LLC
Chambersburg PA
CBHW070350300526
45791CB00025B/1812